THE LEADING
EDGE

9 STRATEGIES FOR IMPROVING INTERNAL
AND INTENTIONAL LEADERSHIP

Drs. Steve & Rebecca Wilke

The Leading Edge: 9 Strategies for Improving Internal and Intentional Leadership
Copyright ©2010 Drs. Steve and Rebecca Wilke
All rights reserved

Cover Design by Gary Christensen
Interior Design by Pine Hill Graphics
Editor Hannah Selleck

Library of Congress Cataloging-in-Publication Data
(Provided by Cassidy Cataloguing Services, Inc.)

Wilke, Steve (Stephen D.)

   The leading edge : 9 strategies for improving internal and intentional
   leadership / Steve & Rebecca Wilke. -- 1st ed. -- San Diego, CA :
   LEADon, 2010.

      p. ; cm.

      ISBN: 978-0-615-33343-4
      Includes bibliographical references.

         1. Leadership. 2. Organizational effectiveness.
      3. Organizational change. 4. Personnel management.
      5. Management. I. Wilke, Rebecca Lynn. II. Title.

HD57.7 .W524 2010
658.4/092--dc22   1004

Printed in the United States of America.

Table of Contents

Preface

No matter the status of the market, savvy business people know they need an edge on the competition. This edge provides the narrow margin necessary to pass by, move in on, and beat out all the others, much like what race car drivers do in order to be at the head of the pack. All competitors, whether for NASCAR or for the bread factory in town, will look for that edge—wait for that edge—then take advantage of that edge to increase their chances of winning.

Think about any sport you enjoy. Having an edge on the competition is always part of a successful team's strategy. If a runner or swimmer better prepares for an event than fellow competitors, he or she will more than likely win the race. When a football team takes time to scout the opposing players, sometimes spending hours on end watching game film, that preparation greatly increases the odds of a victory.

And what about life outside of sports? Preparation and planning can offer you an edge in many situations. For instance, when you take time to investigate the best rates for a car or home loan, the final deal tends to tip in your favor instead of the bank's. If someone takes time to study and attain an advanced degree, he or she has an advantage over the competition when entering the job market.

It's the American way to plan and prepare in order to attain better and brighter futures, but even when we plan well, sometimes we take a hit from something we can't control. Our marketplace has taken some substantial hits the past few years. We've all taken some hits—and they've hurt. It may even seem that getting ahead is nearly impossible any more.

But we're here to tell you that you can still attain the edge in life. In fact, we are confident that the principles we're going to share with you in *The Leading Edge: 9 Strategies for Improving Internal and Intentional Leadership* will help restore your hope that greatness is truly possible. We will mentor you through these strategies, as team managers or coaches mentor their players. We want to take you on a journey you may never have experienced before, one that will provide new ideas to contemplate, new strategies to implement, and new roads to profitability and productivity. By the way, this profitability will not simply be defined by profit and losses—it will also be measured by employee and customer satisfaction, team cohesion, increased knowledge and skills sets, and long-term legacy. You'll discover that productivity is more than just a product; high performance, stronger rapport between team members, innovativeness, creativity, entrepreneurialism, and group genius will be some of the additional tangible and intangible results of this straight line process.

Part I of *The Leading Edge* introduces Personal Strategies for success that should profoundly impact you for the rest of your life. Books on business seldom deal with the personal aspects of leadership; instead, they tend to focus on the bottom line. Our belief is that the foundation for all success must begin with personal leadership choices. Once we coach you through some strategies to improve who you are as an individual, you'll be more than prepared to build on these principles in your professional life, too.

Professional Strategies is the spotlight of Part II of *The Leading Edge*. Our goal is to encourage you to become an exceptional leader—someone who makes such a difference in your organization that your legacy will become legendary! We'll offer some unique insights that will assist you in fielding a "Hall of Fame" team. Then we'll give you guidelines on how to develop and maintain your team so that you'll not only get the edge on the competition, but you'll also experience measurable increases in productivity and profitability.

In the final chapters of *The Leading Edge*, the emphasis is on refining your Team Strategies. You will learn specific skills to combat and remove the barriers to greatness in your business. We'll guide you through the concept of Corporate Culture, presenting ideas about how to relate to your employees as part of a "Corporate Family." Part III will also motivate you to get your team aligned and attuned despite generational differences so that everyone feels comfortable with accountability—which leads to significant success.

After working with numerous executives, teams, and organizations across the country, we know that the principles we share with you in this book are practical and essential for your success in all aspects of life. Are you willing to travel down this exciting road with us? The strategies that follow will help guide you on this journey; all you have to do is start putting them into practice as we work together to attain *The Leading Edge* that you've been looking for!

Acknowledgments

Our journey through leadership development has been greatly enriched by the lives of many men and women who have taken time to mentor and coach us in our personal lives and professional experiences. A debt of gratitude goes out to our family members, teachers, professors, and colleagues who have added invaluably to who we are today. We have also learned much from our LEADon, Inc. clients. Thank you all for making a difference in the lives of others!

We are also deeply grateful to the following individuals for their efforts in helping *The Leading Edge* reach its final format:

Dr. Stuart Gothold, clinical professor emeritus at the University of Southern California, for your insights into the needs of leaders in the 21st century.

Dr. Ron Jenson, chairman and co-founder of Future Achievement International, for your expertise on coaching and mentoring as well as principle-based leadership.

Dave Raspolich, for giving LEADon opportunities to implement principle-based leadership across the country.

Ryan Wilke, for your intensive research and editing even while working on your medical degree.

Jared Wilke, for your assistance at LEADon, particularly in understanding the needs of Millennials in today's workplace.

Teri Cowling, our executive assistant, for your organizational skill sets which are in a class of their own.

Gary Christenson, graphic designer and photographer, for our cover concept and artistic input at LEADon, Inc.

Hannah Selleck, from DoubleCheck Editing, whose expertise and editorial skills perfected the final format of this book.

Fred Renich, from Pine Hill Graphics, for your technical and production skills that put the finishing touches on *The Leading Edge*.

Successful Leaders
Need Straight Lines

Never has a man who has bent himself been able to make others straight.

Mencius, 372—289 B.C.

S everal years ago we received a call from Ben Sumner, CEO of Bantham Industrial Supplies* a manufacturing company in a large metropolitan city. After a brief discussion about his concerns, Ben Sumner set up a visit with us at Bantham. Ben told us the main reason for seeking our help was that his company had been experiencing losses with no sign of improvement.

We arrived at Bantham early one Monday morning, eager to meet with the executive team and begin to assess the needs of this 100-year-old business. Ben greeted us at the door of

---

*Many names have been changed in this book for confidentiality.

the corporate headquarters and swiftly led us to his office for a private conversation before meeting the team.

"I didn't want to go into too much detail on the phone," Ben began after introductions were made, "but we've got some real problems here. I've been in charge for the past five years, but many of the employees have been here fifteen to twenty. I'm so frustrated with the attitude around here; I've told everyone from the executive team down that if they would just do the right thing, we could turn things around."

After fifteen minutes of animated conversation, Ben escorted us to a conference room where we were introduced to the members of the executive team. After spending thirty minutes with them, a major part of the problem at Bantham became apparent. The organizational chart, if you could even call it that, looked more like a drawing on an Etch-A- Sketch. All of the leaders in the room had titles, but very few could clearly express what his or her roles and responsibilities were.

When we met with the management team after lunch, we discovered virtually the same chaotic mess in Bantham's "organization." In addition, when Sumner was out of the room on a conference call, many of these employees shared that they weren't sure why their CEO tended to "rant and rave" about doing "the right thing." They all thought they were doing the right thing; after all, they came to work each day, completed their tasks, and tried to fulfill their roles—though they struggled with exactly what these were. As for accountability—well, let's just say there wasn't any system in place other than Ben's occasional, "motivational" speeches. No clearly defined standard existed for individual or company-wide accountability.

The finishing detail of our assessment of Bantham came as we were wrapping things up with the executive team. When we asked how many quarters they had been suffering losses, the CFO piped up from the back of the room:

"Forty."

"Forty?" we asked in disbelief.

All nine executives, including the CEO, nodded.

Now, we're not sure about how you would respond, but if LEADon suffered *two* quarters of loses, we'd be concerned—big time! And if that trend continued another quarter, our leadership team would have gone into high-alert, full emergency mode to find the problem and fix it.

Yet this company—a 100-year-old business with a previously winning record in a competitive market place—waited until they were *forty quarters* in the red before seeking professional help.

Unfortunately, we've discovered many companies that struggle like Bantham in just about every industry, though none have matched their ten year losing streak! In addition to an unwillingness to seek help, some leaders simply don't recognize that they too have areas that need to be drastically improved. Ben Sumner, while professional in appearance and attitude, didn't realize the basis for the chaos in his company—he had failed to establish clear roles and responsibilities, even for his key executives. No system for accountability was in place to encourage success within his team. Instead of addressing these issues, he reverted to how he'd probably been treated when things didn't work right: he ranted about the incompetence of his employees.

> If we had to net their problem out, we'd summarize by saying that Bantham Industrial Supplies simply had no *straight lines* in place to guide its employees anywhere.

If we had to net their problem out, we'd summarize by saying that Bantham Industrial Supplies simply had no *straight lines* in place to guide its employees anywhere.

STRAIGHT LINES TO SUCCESS

You may be asking what we mean by straight lines. Straight lines are more than guidelines; they are clear boundaries that give purpose and bearing. They include roles and responsibilities, but they also offer direction which encourages forward motion and progress. In an organization, this includes not only a position title, but also specific job descriptions and expectations which correspond to that title. A company that doesn't provide clarity will find itself in a situation just like that of Bantham—disorganized, chaotic, and trending toward the red.

We see examples of straight lines at work in the real world each and every day. Boundaries between neighbors allow us to have privacy and protection. The laws of the road are written in straight lines, and fewer accidents occur when we stay within those lines. In addition, drivers have roles and responsibilities which foster everyone's safe passage. The buildings we live and work in are structurally sound thanks to straight lines; some curves here and there add beauty and variation, but it's the parallel and perpendicular lines that offer the majority of the support.

> The straight line is the standard—it is what all other shapes and forms can be measured against.

Socrates has been quoted as saying that people won't know a line is crooked until they put a straight line next to it. The straight line is the standard—it is what all other shapes and forms can be measured against. As Mencius pointed out, it's also impossible for men and women to help straighten others out when they aren't modeling that approach themselves!

The family unit is a practical example of this straight line philosophy benefitting everyone involved. Each member of the family has specific roles. A youngster should realize that it's not his or her job to tell the parent what to do; likewise, parents understand it's their responsibility to give direction to children.

Family members also have specific responsibilities. They know when they need to get up each morning, what they should do to get ready for their day, and where they must be by a certain time. In addition, they know the consequences of not meeting those basic guidelines. For instance, if you don't get up and go to work, the bills won't get paid. If your child chooses not to go to school, you have consequences in place for that decision—such as grounding or taking away privileges.

> The main reason for clarity in these roles and responsibilities is so that the objectives of the entire corporate family can be met.

The "Corporate Family" shouldn't be any different. Each member needs set directives for his or her role in the company as well as specific help in understanding his or her exact responsibilities to the company and to others in the business. The main reason for clarity in these roles and responsibilities is so that the objectives of the entire corporate family can be met. In a professional family, one of the chief responsibilities of the "parents" (the executive team members) is to provide those straight lines.

> Straight lines are neither unrealistic nor idealistic.

Also, straight lines are neither unrealistic nor idealistic, but they are *absolutely necessary* within the climate and culture in which we live and do business. We need them in order to be personally successful. Professionally, they're critical for achieving our goals and competing in the global economy. And teams, from individual families to corporations, cannot survive—let alone thrive—without them.

A CLOSER LOOK AT LEADERSHIP

At the time we were writing this book, the United States and the world were in the midst of one of the most serious economic crises in modern history. Many experts believed that the failure of key leaders—from Washington to Wall Street—to follow basic tenets of integrity and honesty was the root of the financial calamity. In other words, these leaders—whether elected officials, governance appointees, or corporate leaders—ultimately ignored standards of character, ethics, and sound judgment. Many strayed from these straight lines, while others turned their backs on them completely for their own financial benefit or political gain.

The straight lines we're discussing are in contrast to the postmodern principles and values prevalent in today's society. Indeed, the entire dilemma of 2008 to 2009 might be called the "Postmodern Economic Crash." Postmodernism in the late 20th and early 21st century describes a distrust of theories and ideologies, and its "initial concern is to de-naturalize some of the dominant features of our way of life" (Hutcheon, 2002, p. 2). This rebellion of postmodern thinking led to a questioning of authority, looser definitions, and even looser boundaries for everything from art to politics to social philosophy.

The bottom line of the "Postmodern Economic Crash" is that the key players in society did what seemed best for them at the time, regardless of business and moral ethics. Yet adherence to the traditional principles and values of American culture might have spared us the terrible consequences of the market falling, investments dwindling, home equity plummeting, and unemployment escalating. In other words, this crash was avoidable if simple straight lines had been followed by our leaders.

This dreadful decision-making process was unfortunately aided by the relative-based, pluralistic environment we are all living in. It's becoming increasingly difficult to set straight lines because many people suggest that we should just let everyone do what they think is best. Yet how has this way of thinking ever worked out for you? What would your family be like if each member did only what he or she wanted? Imagine what would happen in your company: how productive would you be if you allowed employees to do as they pleased? After all, we don't want to step on anyone's toes—right?

> What works, however, are clearly defined straight lines that offer freedom as long as everyone operates within them in a committed and consistent manner.

Wrong! In business, relativity can lead to chaos and bankruptcy. *What works, however, are clearly defined straight lines that offer freedom as long as everyone operates within them in a committed and consistent manner.* Then, if you add to the straight lines a dose of mutual accountability, you will get a sense of the success everyone will experience.

Since we are talking about straight lines, we'd like to spend a few minutes discussing the difference between success and significance as affected by leadership. Many times success is measured in numbers—bottom line figures at the end of a spread sheet. You may be surprised to find out that this type of success is not the only judge of great leadership. Exceptional leaders also impact people in a way that leads to lasting, quantifiable results; this is what significance is all about. Their employees want their leaders' input; they beg for their insights. Most clamor for their directives because they know those guidelines will lead to everyone's success. These types of leaders are so significant personally and professionally that people cry when they leave or retire, and the legacy of these individuals keeps those who remain behind going and growing!

Compare your significance to an executive we knew at a large, financially successful company. This CEO was mean, ruthless, yet extremely wealthy from the annual bonuses he received from year-after-year record profits. One day when a car wreck happened close by corporate headquarters, employees stopped work, turned on the news, and wondered out loud to one another if they'd be lucky enough to attend their CEO's funeral in a few days. Shocking? Absolutely! This businessman had plenty of financial success, but everyone, from his leadership team down, hated him.

Now we're not saying that there's anything wrong with winning. Winning is what having the leading edge is all about! We believe in achieving the "Blue Ribbon" and that setting your sights any lower than this is underachieving. High Performance Teams (HPTs) strive for first place, the gold medal, and status in the Hall of Fame.

> Straight line standards are not only defined by exceptional leaders but they are also lived out—first personally, then professionally!

So win—and win big! But don't strive to win at all costs—especially at the cost of your integrity or the loss of respect by those around you. Straight line standards are not only defined by exceptional leaders but they are also lived out—first personally, then professionally!

Speaking of winning, you may be wondering about Bantham Industrial Supplies. After all, the chief executive finally took the initiative to seek assistance and improve his leadership skills, so they had wildly positive results, right? Unfortunately, this was far from the case.

You see, as much as Ben Sumner wanted to make progress, he wasn't willing to put in the work necessary to make those critical changes and attain the leading edge. He talked big but failed to take the journey much farther down the road. Ben Sumner is the example of an executive who used words without actions so that the results were futile and unsuccessful; similarly, reading this book without putting its principles into action each and every day would be just as pointless.

Here are some of the main problems that Ben and everyone at Bantham faced:

+ Incompetent people in the wrong positions.
+ No clearly defined roles and responsibilities for leaders or their subordinates.
+ Poor direction from executive leadership.
+ No shared accountability within the organization.
+ Rampant, unrealistic expectations.
+ Complete resistance by those in leadership to correct any of these.

> Good leaders influence in positive, productive ways that leave a legacy that's better than when they arrived.

If leadership is about influence, this company is an example of how bad leadership influenced what should have been a productive organization. Bad leaders have a negative, destructive impact; *good leaders influence in positive, productive ways that leave a legacy that's better than when they arrived.* Ben Sumner made a great move by finally getting some help, but after a few months, he decided to go back to the system that Bantham had been using for years. He wanted to keep trying to bring the business back into the black on his own. He'd been provided with the 9 Straight Line Strategies that we're going to share with you in order to help his corporate family attain the leading edge it needed in a competitive market place, but he chose not to continue the process of improving internal and intentional leadership.

A NEW JOURNEY

Fortunately Ben Sumner is the exception, not the rule. In our work with thousands of executives across the country, we've found many men and women who have been more than willing to hear new insights, try different strategies, and continually strive toward successful leadership for themselves and their teams. These leaders have not only gone "from good to great," (Collins, 2001) but also from surviving to thriving! They are winners, and their winning teams are so committed to their vision that they want to follow these leaders as they work to create something new and exciting.

In the upcoming chapters we're going to carefully guide you through the 9 Straight Line Strategies that will help you improve your performance through *internal* and *intentional* leadership. Here are the strategies we plan to address:

Chapter 2 - Straight Line #1:
Standards for Hall of Fame Leadership

Chapter 3 - Straight Line #2:
Six Benchmarks for Internal and Intentional Leadership

Chapter 4 - Straight Line #3:
Discover Personal and Professional Life Balance

Chapter 5 - Straight Line #4:
Field Your High Performance Team

Chapter 6 - Straight Line #5:
Develop Your High Performance Team

Chapter 7 - Straight Line #6:
Maintain Your High Performance Team

Chapter 8 - Straight Line #7:
Lead the Generations

Chapter 9 - Straight Line #8:
Corporate Culture Always Impacts the Bottom Line

Chapter 10 - Straight Line #9:
Leave a Lasting Legacy through Internal and Intentional Leadership

As we close this first chapter, we are offering you a choice about how you want to proceed from here. As you've probably already figured out, this journey toward exceptional leadership will not be an easy one, and it's certainly not for the faint-hearted. There is nothing soft about this initiative!

But know this: if you choose to travel down this road, we promise to be with you every step of the way. We've seen numerous success stories, and we can assure you that improvement in your personal and professional performance will be natural results of this process. You can get that leading edge through your internal and intentional leadership. Let's start the next leg of the journey by looking at the personal strategies that will lead to success and significance in all that you do.

SHARPENING YOUR EDGE

Choose one or more of these action items to sharpen your edge today.

1. List five "straight lines" that guide you in your personal life. (How do you spend your free time? How do you take care of your health? How much time do you spend with your family?)

2. Now think about your professional life. Write five "straight lines" that you won't compromise on when it comes to what you do in your career. Post these two lists somewhere you'll see them, and reflect on them as you read *The Leading Edge*.

3. How would you like to improve as a leader? List four of the most important areas that you would like to address while reading this book. Force rank these in order of importance so you can focus on improving these short-term goals. (Note: We would expect this list might change as you work through *The Leading Edge*).

4. What kind of legacy do you intend to leave behind? Who will take your place? Are you cascading transformational leadership that will ensure the kind of legacy you can be proud of? Make a list of the specific ways you are cascading leadership as part of your professional life.

Part I

3 PERSONAL STRATEGIES

Hall of Fame Leadership

*His name was familiar to government and people, to
kings, courtiers, nobility, clergy, and philosophers, as well
as plebeians, to such a degree that there was scarcely a
peasant or citizen…who did not consider him as a friend
of humankind.*

John Adams writing about Benjamin Franklin, c. 1778

Who in modern-day America isn't familiar with the
name Benjamin Franklin? He is recognized as one of
the founders of the United States. He was an author, printer,
political theorist, scientist, inventor, and statesman. Creator
of the first public library in America, he also is credited with
inventing the lightning rod, bifocals, the Franklin stove, and
the carriage odometer. Interestingly enough, he was no less
famous in the late 18th century. As John Adams wrote so can-
didly, Franklin was beloved by everyone—from kings to ordinary citizens. According to one historian, "his likeness appeared
everywhere—in prints, on medallions, on the lids of snuff

boxes—making his face, as Franklin himself said, as well known as that of the man in the moon" (McCullough, 2001, p. 193).

The end of the Adam's quote provides one of the best insights into his worldwide acclaim and overwhelming admiration: *people considered Franklin a friend of humankind.* There was something about his personality, his interactions with others, and his compassion that struck a chord with those around him. So beloved was this "representative American" that, according to McCullough, "crowds in the streets cheered the 'good doctor'" (pp. 193—4).

In LEADon terminology, we'd say that Benjamin Franklin had discovered the secret to Hall of Fame Leadership. Individuals who belong to this Hall of Fame aren't just superstars in their area of expertise or technical skill set. That type of specialization involves IQ (Intelligence Quotient) and training in a particular field or profession. For instance, you may be outstanding in your industry, but that doesn't guarantee that you've mastered every skill necessary to become an exceptional leader—especially when we include personal and professional "straight line" standards.

In this chapter, we're going to be discussing specific personal strategies that are necessary to attain the leading edge in your life. IQ helps determine how you perform vocationally, but it only accounts for 1/6 of the overall "DNA" to Hall of Fame Leadership. In addition to IQ, there are five characteristics that leaders must focus on in order to completely, successfully, and significantly impact their world. These five attributes fall into a category called EQ.

EQ MAKES ALL THE DIFFERENCE

What exactly is EQ? EQ stands for Emotional Quotient, or our level of emotional intelligence. EQ includes, "self-control, zeal, and persistence, and the ability to motivate oneself" (Goleman, 1994, p. xii). Our abilities in the area of EQ impact how we relate to the people in our world, and how others relate to us. In fact, in their book *Primal Leadership* (2002), Goleman, Boyatzis, and McKee explain that our emotional intelligence is *more important* than intellectual intelligence when it comes to professional and personal success.

> Our abilities in the area of EQ impact how we relate to the people in our world, and how others relate to us.

Put another way, EQ has to do with your interpersonal (social) and intrapersonal (self-awareness) skill sets. Interpersonal intelligence describes how you relate to others; we might call these your social capabilities. Can you communicate with people, understand them, and motivate them? Do you work cooperatively with others? Highly successful individuals tend to connect and interact with people extremely well. In addition, those with great EQ understand who they are as individuals and are quite comfortable in their own skin. These men and women spend time intrapersonally in self-reflection and self-evaluation, using the findings from this introspection to improve themselves.

In terms of your personal and professional leadership, understanding all six characteristics of Hall of Fame Leadership can profoundly impact your life. Let's break them down:

1. *Technical Skills:* taking your training (trade school, professional school, college, graduate school, etc.), credentials, and skill sets and using these to meet the goals and objectives of your business plan.
2. *Leadership:* providing your team and corporate family members with motivation, guidance and support, and being able to communicate a common goal.

3. *Culture:* creating an environment where the Values, Beliefs, and Behavior Patterns of the corporate family will support the objectives of the business plan.

4. *Competence:* merging you and your team members' technical knowledge and EQ skills to provide results to the business plan. In other words, combining IQ and EQ so that positive results can occur.

5. *Commitment:* proving that you can reliably support your team's objectives through consistent action, effort, and motivation.

6. *EQ:* mastering, modeling, and mentoring the interpersonal and intrapersonal skill sets we call "Emotional Quotient."

Items two through six may appear to be a bit "soft science" to some. It's true; there aren't as many tests or standard methods to measure the results of these traits when compared to the first characteristic. Technical ability can be evaluated in terms of IQ tests, grades on exams, scores in courses taken, certification or degrees granted from programs or colleges, etc. Yet the five additional characteristics account for 5/6 of the skills needed by leaders in order to truly make it into the Hall of Fame of leadership, especially in today's multi-faceted, global economy.

> **EQ wins over IQ every time!**

Spend a few moments considering how many people either have been trained or are being educated in some area of technical expertise. There are more trade schools, colleges, and universities in America than ever before in history, and access to these institutions is also at an unprecedented level. We have plenty of smart and highly trained people! *What we desperately need are individuals who can get along with others, be team players, fit into the culture of our corporations, lead when no one else is watching, and care about the overall good of co-workers and their company.* EQ wins over IQ every time!

All of those attributes describe a man or woman who is competent in the areas of emotional intelligence. Soft? Maybe to some people, but we can assure you that addressing the EQ skill sets will be some of the toughest work leaders will ever do. However, the effort put into improving emotional intelligence will pay off in increased satisfaction and success over the long term.

It's also important to note that these five attributes can be observed in both the personal and professional aspects of an individual's life. You can be technically savvy at work, but you don't have to be so at home. On the other hand, you can't be a leader only when you're on the job. *Leadership skills transcend time and place.* A person

> Leadership skills transcend time and place.

who has high levels of commitment demonstrates this reality to everyone he or she interacts with, not just with co-workers. Cultural awareness and sensitivity won't simply be noticed from 9 a.m. to 5 p.m. Men and women who radiate emotional intelligence positively impact every part of their world, personally first, then professionally.

Many of the founding fathers understood what Franklin lived out. Other dedicated men and women believed that good leadership began with self-leadership. Their willingness to focus on their personal character, integrity, commitment, and competence allowed others to be motivated by their examples and become willing to follow them into the battle despite any dismal forecasts for success. No one cared about George Washington's IQ level—they were inspired by his ability to lead. It was Jefferson's commitment to his words that spoke to the populace. *It was these leaders of the United States' EQ, rather than IQ, that inspired people and rallied them to strive for victory.*

LEADING THE EQ WAY

Society and culture impact our emotional development and our ability to understand ourselves and relate to others. Most of us have learned our emotional intelligence capabilities through our life experiences—from our families, friends, and social connections. Looking at these sources of emotional education, we can see that many have the potential to be dysfunctional at best and, at worst, pathological.

> It was these leaders of the United States' EQ, rather than IQ, that inspired people and rallied them to strive for victory.

Think about your own experiences growing up in your family of origin (the family that raised you)—how would you rate your parents' emotional quotient? Did your mom relate well with others and help you do the same, or was she introverted, shy, maybe avoidant? How about your dad? Was he able to be introspective and then assist you in learning how to figure out who you are? Think about your friends, the neighborhood, and the city you grew up in, and the cultural influences you had while you were growing up. How did those elements impact the way you think about yourself and interact with others today?

Suffice it to say that many of us probably lacked mentoring when it came to leadership, cultural awareness, competence, and commitment skills—all of which are mandatory characteristics to the DNA of Hall of Fame Leadership. These same skill sets are where personal and professional battles are won or lost.

If you are wondering if you can ever change your current ability, based on a lifetime of learning good—and not-so-good—emotional skill sets, we've got great news. *You can improve EQ! Unlike IQ, EQ is malleable.* Your strengths in the areas of interpersonal and intrapersonal intelligences can be built upon. The weaknesses that you've known about or are just becoming aware of can be improved if you're willing to do some *internal* and *intentional* work.

> These same skill sets are where personal and professional battles are won or lost.

We've observed improvement in EQ as we've worked with leaders across the nation. Many of these executives, managers, and team leaders had amazing technical skills—they are "first in class" type of people. But as far as relating to their subordinates—well, let's just say they were found wanting. When their co-workers were asked about their leaders' ability to "build a fierce loyalty by caring about the careers of those who work for them and inspire people to give their best" (Goleman, Boyatzis, & McKee, 2002, p. 248), many were given negative reviews. Yet when they began focusing on the five characteristics we've been sharing with you, everyone around them noted marked

> You can improve EQ! Unlike IQ, EQ is malleable.

improvement, and their continued growth in these areas have enhanced their personal and professional lives.

ERIK'S STORY

Perhaps we can best summarize these positive transformations by sharing the story of one leader who desperately needed help and finally had the opportunity to receive it—he was given an ultimatum to do so or else be fired (not the kind of incentive for change that we'd usually recommend, but in this case it was effective).

Erik Harrison was referred to us by the executive team at his organization. Erik had been hired right out of college with lots of potential for leadership. He certainly had exceptional technical skills, which was one of the chief reasons he'd been hired in the first place. However, little evaluation was done by the company to determine if Erik also had sufficient ability in the other five Hall of Fame Leadership attributes.

Erik did quite well during the first six months at his new company, even receiving a promotion at his mid-year evaluation as well as a corresponding raise in salary. However, during the second half of that year, Erik's co-workers and his supervisor began to observe changes in his behavior and interactions in the workplace. Angry outbursts were some of the first problems noted, including several hostile encounters with another colleague during and after work hours. To make matters worse, a client called to complain, stating that he never wanted to work with Erik again. This client concluded by saying, "If Mr. Harrison's poor attitude is representative of your company, we may never do business with it again either."

Once we had a chance to meet with Erik, we discovered that his personal life wasn't in any better shape. He'd been angry and more volatile at home; he felt this was in part due to his and his wife's frustration about not being able to have children. His wife's job had become more demanding as well, so they both were spending many hours at work and less time together. As part of his own stress-reduction plan, Erik had begun drinking more than he ever had before.

The bottom line was fairly simple: his personal life and professional life were a complete mess, and the stress Erik was feeling from these failures was at the highest level imaginable. Despite his great IQ and outstanding technical skills, Erik was struggling emotionally. As we shared these truths with Erik, we also suggested that he appeared to be at a crossroad in life—one that would determine what the future would hold for him. In addition, we reminded him that the good news about this crossroad is that choices about direction in life can be made. Did he truly want to fix his personal and professional dilemmas or not? Was he willing to put in time and effort to get things back on track?

Erik chose the road leading to positive change. He realized that he would lose everything—his new job and his wife—if he didn't do something immediately. So together we developed a specific plan to help Erik get back on the right path. Here are the steps Erik was to follow:

+ Erik would begin working with us on specific Executive Coaching strategies.
+ Erik would stop drinking and get help for his substance abuse and anger management issues.
+ Erik and his wife would go to couple's counseling for several months.
+ Erik would begin targeting the EQ skill sets that he struggled in and read several books we recommended on emotional intelligence.
+ Erik would keep a daily record on his attempts at work and at home to implement all six of the Hall of Fame Leadership components.

Notice that each step begins with "Erik." Erik is the one who needed to make these choices, take personal responsibility, and attempt to change the situation he was in. He wouldn't have improved if he'd blamed his wife, co-workers, or boss. The ball was in his court—and his court only—and the straight lines for success were now clearly laid out.

Despite his weaknesses, Erik was highly motivated to improve his personal and professional life. He not only intentionally implemented the strategies above, but he also exceeded his own expectations, receiving a glowing report at his next evaluation meeting. He and his wife had made great strides to repair their relationship, and they were spending much more time together, balancing their busy work schedules and prioritizing their marriage. The greatest compliment and confirmation of the positive transformation came at the end of Erik's second year with the company. The client who had previously complained about Erik's poor attitude and performance contacted one of the executive team members and reported, "We've decided that we won't do work with your company *unless* Mr. Harrison is on our team."

The significant changes that Erik made were noticed by everyone in his life. You can't put a number value on restored relationships, and it would be next to impossible to specifically calculate how improvement in one employee benefited the company as a whole. However, workplace conflict was down and productivity up. Clients weren't offended; instead, they were committed. Because of the executive team's belief in developing leadership skill sets, they ended up not only with the great technically-skilled employee they'd hired, but also one whose EQ growth positively impacted everyone around him.

THE WAY TO THE HALL OF FAME

Compare this success story to another business we encountered. Monica Morales contacted us one spring about concerns she had for her regional team. Communication was poor between the leaders, partly due to the distant locations of each business in different cities. Monica had been striving for several months to bring leaders in her region together, and they finally arranged a day-long session when most of them could meet at her worksite.

Ms. Morales requested that, after the presentation, we facilitate some team-building activities. Also, we planned a curriculum that would help them improve their communication skills and specifically target conflict resolution. As the day progressed, we were pleased with the interactions of the group members. They participated in all activities and had good discussions about the content we covered. Yet, when we asked for their feedback at the end of the day, about half of the leaders responded that they wished they'd spent more time on talking about business matters. In fact, they really wanted to see more business examples in the materials next time we spoke to them.

When the session concluded, we decided to look back over the information we'd covered with this group, thinking we had missed something. After reviewing our notes and getting additional feedback from Ms. Morales, we finally figured out the problem. It wasn't that there hadn't

> The dilemma was that these leaders were clamoring for more information about technical and IQ skills when what they really needed was help with their EQ skill sets.

been enough connection to business—business examples had been embedded everywhere! We had talked about their organization throughout the day and referenced examples of several other companies as we shared. The dilemma was that these leaders were clamoring for more information about technical and IQ skills when what they really needed was help with their

EQ skill sets. Without even knowing it, they were resisting the very thing we had been called to help them with: improving their ability to relate to and interact with one another.

The resistance of this group is not unusual. Indeed, you may be struggling with some of the concepts that we've been sharing. After all, technical programs and business courses rarely discuss your interpersonal and intrapersonal intelligences. When did mentors, professors, or bosses sit down and talk about how improving your EQ skills might enhance your professional abilities? That makes these ideas new, unusual, and even daunting.

Leadership experts such as Rosenbach and Taylor (2006) as well as Cherniss and Goleman (2001) report that 90% of star performers differ from the average in senior leadership positions due to their emotional intelligence rather than intellectual abilities. This alone should encourage you to consider the benefits that improved EQ may have in your life.

Based on our work with leaders, we can safely say that *internally* and *intentionally* developing these five characteristics of the DNA of Hall of Fame Leadership are important for these reasons:

+ You will experience dramatic improvement in your personal and professional life.
+ You will improve operational efficiency.
+ You will be able to build High Performance Teams.
+ You will select and maintain top talent.
+ You will improve the quality of key leaders throughout your organization.

Many organizations are now utilizing LEADon's "straight line" guidelines for the DNA of Hall of Fame Leadership in the hiring process. We often tell leaders that you should be able to toss the resume out on the day you interview someone. The technical skills of the potential employee should be known at this point in the process. Instead, those precious minutes of the interview can be better spent evaluating that individual's level of emotional intelligence. How does he or she interact with you or others on the interview committee? Does he or she have good communication skills, eye contact, and introspective insights to the questions being asked? What are his or her strengths in terms of leadership, cultural awareness, competence, and commitment? Do you get a sense that this person has strong emotional intelligence, or does something seem to be lacking?

This type of EQ evaluation is also important to include in operational reviews and evaluations of your employees. They aren't "soft skills;" they provide straight lines to encourage employee growth and development. They may help you avoid potential Human Resource problems down the road by identifying trouble spots so you can supply assistance—much like Erik Harrison's leaders did. Most importantly, LEADon's Hall of Fame attributes offer you excellent self-evaluation tools as you strive to attain the leading edge in your personal and professional life.

SHARPENING YOUR EDGE

1. Consider your level of emotional intelligence. On a scale of 1-10 (1 as low, 10 as high), how would you rate your Emotional Quotient (EQ)? What score would your family members give you? What score would your vocational sphere of influence give you? What score would your clients give you?

2. The DNA of Hall of Fame Leadership includes the following skill sets that need to be developed into professional habits:
   + Technical
   + Leadership
   + Culture
   + Competence
   + Commitment
   + EQ

   Force rank these skill sets from your greatest strength to your greatest need for improvement. Make sure that your peers would agree with your self-evaluation. Write a leadership business plan to improve in any area of need. Share this plan with your mentor and sphere of influence.

4. Finding a mentor who will assist you in improving any significant area of your life is essential for long-term transformation. Become a protégée so that a mentor can hold you accountable to your leadership business plan and can assist you in your professional growth.

5. Review both the recruiting and staff development policies of your organization. How does your corporate family measure up to all six characteristics that comprise the DNA of Hall Of Fame Leadership? Are there any changes that would "sharpen the edge" of your company?

6. Analyze how you and your company hire new employees. Do you look for all six characteristics of the DNA of Hall of Fame Leadership? If not, how can you improve your hiring process?

Chapter T H R E E

Six Benchmarks for Internal and Intentional Leadership

Good leadership consists in showing average people how to do the work of superior people.

John D. Rockefeller

The name Rockefeller is still familiar to many in the 21st century. An American industrialist in the late 19th and early 20th century, John D. Rockefeller made his money in oil. He revolutionized the industry and established the Standard Oil Company, which produced 90% of the oil in America. Driven to achieve something no one had ever done before, Rockefeller bought up businesses, making and breaking the fortunes of those in his path. By the time he retired in 1947, his estimated worth was about 1.5 billion dollars; historians would soon proclaim him as the world's first billionaire (Chernow, 2004). Rockefeller spent the next forty years of his retirement in philanthropic work, giving generously to assist the advancement of medicine, education, and scientific research.

While some historians debate his controversial methods of business (the Standard Oil Company was broken up in the early 20th century because it was considered a monopoly), no one doubts Rockefeller's success as a leader in his industry. His insightful quote provides some intriguing food for thought about successful leadership. In a sense, Rockefeller suggested that there must be a difference between good leaders and average workers, and that average, ordinary individuals need extra attention in order to understand good leadership.

> In reality only a small percentage of people can and do undertake the ultimate responsibility for the leadership of others.

While that doesn't sound very sensitive or "politically correct," we agree with Rockefeller on his premise. Although some men and women would like to think that everyone can be a leader, in reality only a small percentage of people *can* and *do* undertake the ultimate responsibility for the leadership of others. And while we can and should encourage leadership development in our corporations, not everyone will want to assume the roles and responsibilities required of leaders.

For those who do choose to take on this challenge, current leaders and those aspiring to become leaders, then this chapter is for you. We are going to add six new characteristics to help you in your journey toward attaining the leading edge. While the six attributes of the DNA of Hall of Fame Leadership (see Chapter 2) are to be taught to all team members throughout your organization, the following benchmarks are for leaders only. We're going to ask you to build on some skills you already have, try a few new ones on for size, and start putting these benchmarks into action in your personal and professional life. *Everyone on your organizational chart should be working on the DNA of Hall of Fame Leadership, but all leaders must begin implementing the Six Benchmarks for Internal and Intentional Leadership:*

1. *Initiate:* creating opportunities conducive to encouraging and promoting sound leadership.
2. *Communicate:* nurturing each team member's understanding of the objectives and goals of the organization in order to clarify personal roles and responsibilities.
3. *Motivate:* establishing an environment in which people desire to achieve the organization's objectives and goals through personal roles and responsibilities.
4. *Sustain:* keeping momentum moving forward and consistently making appropriate mid-course corrections.
5. *Create Commonality of Purpose:* ensuring the alignment and attunement of the organization and keeping its teams focused on the overall direction and objectives in the spirit of unity.
6. *Exhibit Corporate Character:* exhibiting the highest moral force as is evidenced by positive, patterned personal and professional decisions.

Much like the DNA of Hall of Fame Leadership, these six attributes for leaders are not found on an a-la-carte menu. You can't decide to embrace one or two and ignore the others. *Exceptional leadership is not a multiple choice activity.* These are 24 hours a day, 7 days a week leadership traits that must be implemented in your personal and professional life.

> Exceptional leadership is not a multiple choice activity.

BENCHMARK #1: INITIATE

According to Max Depree, CEO of Herman Miller, Inc., and member of Fortune Magazine's National Business Hall of Fame, the primary responsibility of a leader is to define reality. As a leader, you are the one who must create the opportunities that are going to encourage and promote a culture of sound leadership in your corporation. This is what we mean by initiate. Initiators see the vision and get things going. They are unwilling to let their team members stay stagnant; they abhor the status quo. Ronald Reagan once defined it this way: "Status quo...you know, that is Latin for 'the mess we're in.'" And he was right! When leaders let things go, turn a blind eye, or allow poor performance to slide, the business will soon experience problems. Remember Bantham's forty quarter drop? The CEO ignored the problem rather than initiating change—and by the time he decided to get things back on track, just about every aspect of the company was in chaos.

> "Status quo...you know, that is Latin for 'the mess we're in.'"

Whether a leader runs a construction company, a pharmaceutical research lab, or a law firm, this benchmark for exceptional leadership is essential to success. You can begin initiating by simply scheduling and holding meetings where your team can have face time with you. During these group sessions, you can share your vision, help develop the culture of your corporation, resolve conflict, and problem solve. Whatever is on the agenda, be sure that you create opportunities to develop sound leadership by your words as well as by your example.

BENCHMARK #2: COMMUNICATE

Remember what we discussed in Chapter 2 about EQ skills? We acquire much of our Emotional Intelligence as we grow up—from our families, communities, cultural experiences, and other interactions along life's journey. We then take those skills, including communication skills, into our adult lives and corporate families. Interestingly enough, despite all of the modern methods for communication available today, many executives and their teams still struggle to communicate. In part this is because basic communication is an interpersonal skill, and if that skill set is lacking, then every aspect of our lives is impacted.

> Communication comes from the Latin "comminico," which means to share, give, take counsel, join, unite, or participate; the definition implies that these actions would be done with another person.

Communication comes from the Latin "comminico," which means to share, give, take counsel, join, unite, or participate; the definition implies that these actions would be done with another person. As an exceptional leader, one of your main jobs is to communicate well with all of your team members. This doesn't mean you have to be an outstanding orator. No one expects you to speak like Martin Luther King, Jr. or John F. Kennedy, but if all members of your team understand how they are to execute their roles and responsibilities in your company, they will think you are an excellent communicator. If everyone under your leadership fully understands your organization's objectives and how to implement your business plan successfully, then you're meeting the communication benchmark.

If you feel that this is a weak leadership area for you, you're not alone. The majority of leaders struggle with communication at one time or another. When you recognize this is an area of concern, then you've taken the first step to working on the problem. Denial gets you nowhere; acceptance allows for learning to begin. Start by looking at your own team. Does everyone have a clear understanding about roles and responsibilities?

> **Denial gets you nowhere; acceptance allows for learning to begin.**

Harris Interactive and FranklinCovey recently polled 23 thousand U.S. residents employed full time within key industries; in the study, *only one in five workers* said they had a clear "line of sight" between their task and their team's and organization's goals (Covey, 2007). While this statistic seems almost unbelievable, it points to the need for leaders to improve communication skills within their corporate families!

If this is true in your organization, address the problem immediately. Review your company goals and objectives, and make sure each employee knows what they are. Look over your business plan for this year. Is it specific? If not, clarify it; then share it with your entire team. And don't forget, your "home team" is extremely important too. If you aren't communicating well with your family and friends, it's time to rebuild those connections. Spending time sharing, giving, uniting, and participating with these members of your personal life will dramatically improve this critical characteristic of leadership in your professional experiences.

BENCHMARK #3: MOTIVATE

After initiation and communication skills are mastered, you will be ready for the next benchmark: motivate. Every leader has to find ways to help his or her team members *passionately* desire to achieve the team's objectives through their personal roles and responsibilities. We don't often think in terms of "passion" when it comes to business, and yet this is an integral part of success. What company becomes a Fortune 500 member without ardently feeling it has something to offer the public? How can a leader create momentum without passionately believing in the project he or she is working on?

> Every leader has to find ways to help his or her team members passionately desire to achieve the team's objectives through their personal roles and responsibilities.

Think about any motivational speech you've heard. Perhaps you were an athlete and one of your coaches gave a moving, pre-game pep talk that encouraged you and your teammates to go above and beyond the usual competitive experience. Maybe you listened to a famous speaker, preacher, philosopher, politician, or scientist and found yourself moved to change something in your life or in the lives of others.

In business, great leaders will create an environment in which people *desire* to achieve the organization's objectives and goals. Your team members should be passionate about fulfilling their roles and responsibilities. They ought to be zealous when they've got tasks to complete, and each employee

> Your team members should be passionate about fulfilling their roles and responsibilities.

should fervently attempt to lead the company toward increased productivity and profitability. It's been said that leaders who can inspire this kind of grassroots motivation will greatly outperform their competitors every time. As business expert Jim

Collins explains, "if you become the best at something, you'll never remain on top if you don't have intrinsic passion for what you are doing" (2001, p. 97).

We have worked with many companies that are so passionate about what they do that they've printed everything from the mission statement to business slogan on stationary, business cards, corporate vehicles, hats, and T-shirts. In fact, we've run into some of these employees on the weekends wearing their company logos proudly to a ballgame or movie theater. One company even hoisted a banner over the jobsite—forty stories high—to share their inspirational message. They were motivated about sharing their company, and they wanted to pass that passion on to the public.

BENCHMARK #4: SUSTAIN

In life there is a tendency for things to go from active to passive, from forward motion to status quo. This is why it is crucial for leaders to sustain positive, productive momentum in their businesses as well as adjust and make changes whenever necessary in order to accomplish goals and objectives. Exceptional leaders sustain their teams and organizations by keeping momentum moving forward and consistently making mid-course corrections.

> Exceptional leaders sustain their teams and organizations by keeping momentum moving forward and consistently making mid-course corrections.

According to the Second Law of Thermodynamics, everything in nature has a propensity to go from order to disorder unless some sort of energy is put back into the system. For instance, picture your desk at the office. Unless you periodically take time to organize, sort, file, and work on the never ending accumulation of stuff, it won't be long before your desk was a complete disaster.

Businesses aren't any different, and they feel the effects of the lack of effort as well as see it in financial reports. Exceptional leaders know that they must take responsibility for keeping positive and productive momentum going through consistent encouragement and effort. They also realize that sometimes mid-course corrections must be completed, which are often dictated by the marketplace. In order to keep an organization moving forward, there are different decisions that have to be made—by the leaders.

These decisions include *staffing* issues. If demand for your product or services has declined, leaders have to take a look at how that impacts the bottom line and if they must reduce the workforce. *Spending* is another area that leaders must analyze as limiting liabilities on profit and losses and reducing debt impact profitability. The same is true about *capital* since cash is ultimately king in any marketplace. *Sales* are critical, because at the end of the day, you must generate revenue. These are just a sampling of what exceptional leaders must keep an eye on and be willing to change at any time for the good of the team and the organization.

> Leaders must keep momentum going which sometimes involves difficult, even painful, decisions for the organization's ultimate success.

Because of the economic crisis in 2008 and 2009, many U.S. companies have had to make radical mid-course corrections. Organizations reduced the workforces, furloughed employees, implemented salary freezes or reductions, and incorporated massive cost cuts. One executive of a large international firm struggled with these decisions for weeks before finally deciding to have her 1800 employees take a two week furlough. While not popular with everyone on her team, this move saved approximately forty jobs. *The bottom line on sustaining is this: leaders must keep momentum going which sometimes involves difficult, even painful, decisions for the organization's ultimate success.*

BENCHMARK #5:
CREATE COMMONALITY OF PURPOSE

When executives start integrating the first four benchmarks into their skill sets, they often experience positive results relatively quickly. This same impact will be felt when leaders implement the fifth attribute, create commonality of purpose.

> **Leaders are responsible for ensuring the alignment and attunement of all members of their organization.**

Leaders are responsible for ensuring the alignment and attunement of all members of their organization. This process allows teams to keep their focus on the overall direction of the company so they can accomplish individual business objectives in the spirit of unity.

According to a Harris Interactive/FranklinCovey study, *only 37% of employees* surveyed had a clear understanding of what their organization was trying to achieve and why it was attempting to attain it (Covey, 2007). If this is representative of your business, how many individuals in your corporate family actually have a commonality of purpose? *These findings mean that about 63% of your workforce could be off-track, maybe even working against the momentum that you've been trying to create.*

It is possible for you to create commonality of purpose in spite of the situation you may be experiencing right now. Let's spend some time looking at the two key aspects of this benchmark: *alignment* and *attunement*.

Alignment refers to the arrangement of something in a straight line or in an orderly position in relation to something else. As you probably guessed, we like this definition; after all, a straight-line, alignment approach is planned, organized, directional, and intentional. It allows for the purposeful interaction of all parts involved. For instance, a race car driver must have his tires properly positioned so the entire automobile will run at maxim capacity. If even one is out of sync, it doesn't matter how well-positioned the other tires are—the driver doesn't stand a chance of winning.

> We are aligned when we agree.

With people, alignment involves support and alliance. *It's an act of the will—or, better yet, an intellectual choice*; we are aligned when we agree. We choose to work together as a team because we know this will allow for more productivity than working alone. When corporate family members agree to a set of core values, this is an intellectual choice to stay aligned to the same principles.

> Attunement is an act of the heart.

On the other hand, *attunement is an act of the heart;* it means becoming responsive and receptive to others. In music, attunement means harmony and accord. If you've ever heard an instrument that's out of tune (or, even worse, someone who is trying to sing but can't quite keep a tune), you know how you felt—distracted, annoyed, maybe even upset or angry.

Attunement is as critical in your organization as it is to a band, orchestra, or choir. People must be willing to commit to one another in a harmonious manner so that goals and objectives can be attained. This attitude of the heart allows them to put individual differences aside for the greater good of the team. Just because people choose to become part of a team (the intellectual choice—one of alignment) doesn't mean they will be in attunement with the group. They must also emotionally commit to the other team members and be willing to give and take, especially during challenging times.

> We are attuned when we choose to trust and commit.

We are attuned when we choose to trust and commit. This accord in your corporate family will pay off in great dividends down the road. Leaders need to get into the heads and hearts of their subordinates in order to accomplish both alignment and attunement.

If you can create a commonality of purpose among your team members so that they not only buy into (an intellectual decision) but also emotionally commit to (the heart decision) initiatives, your chances for success will be greatly increased. This is the spirit of unity. The choice to be united occurs when everyone puts the team and its objectives before their own needs; then you'll know you're attaining the leading edge which will bring significant success!

BENCHMARK #6: EXHIBIT CORPORATE CHARACTER

We describe this attribute as the highest moral force possible which is evidenced by positive, patterned decisions—both personal and professional. A leader with exceptional corporate character makes decisions based on the most ethical, behavioral, and legal standards possible. If an audit was conducted, leadership history would reveal corporate character to be a standard of practice—or nonexistent.

For example, we often ask executive teams how their employees would respond if queried about the corporate character leaders exhibited. In other words, if we did a character audit on you, how would your co-workers and subordinates talk about you? Would they consider you to be an ethical person or report that your values are of the highest quality?

Consider your home environment, too. Remember, our straight-line philosophy requires that leadership begin at the personal level. What would your spouse or significant other say about your character? Do your kids think of you as a great role model? Do your friends see you as a pillar in the community, or as a constant source of problems?

As a leader, how you support the overall values of your organization will be dictated by your own personal example of corporate character. In their research with companies across the globe, Deal and Kennedy discovered that corporate character is the shared values that "create a sense of identity for those

> This same study revealed that only 28% of the population believed that leaders told the truth.

in the organization…not just the senior executives." (1982, p. 23). Team members will be watching how you exhibit corporate character so they can take ownership of those values too.

It is during times of crises that character is most tested. When leaders—whether in business, education, religion, or politics—waver during these times, people's trust tends to vacillate too. In the 1980s, trust in for-profit companies by the public registered about 60%. That declined to 40% in a survey done in 2000. *This same study revealed that only 28% of the population believed that leaders told the truth* (McKinsey & Company, et al, 2005). Since trust is the heart of corporate character, we have a tremendous amount of rebuilding to do!

Psychologist Albert Ellis helps us get the right perspective on the difficulties of successful leadership: "The best years of your life are the ones in which you decide your problems are your own. You don't blame them on your mother, the ecology, or the president. You realize that you control your own destiny." If you didn't sign up for this, then move aside and let someone else take the lead. However, if you're committed to being an exceptional leader, then embrace the role; take on the challenge enthusiastically. Strive to the finish line, and strive to finish first!

Leslie Murphy chose to embrace her leadership role after 30 years of experience in the building industry. She had started as an intern in a small town company and moved on to run four other businesses. Her current organization was lacking something, in spite of record profits and perceived productivity. She'd been in enough companies to sense that certain leadership components were lacking in key executives, and she knew she needed to fix these before she retired so that the company could continue to run efficiently.

Leslie contacted LEADon and expressed her concerns about the executive team. We targeted three of the six benchmarks that the leaders needed assistance with: communication, commonality of purpose, and corporate character.

Over the next two years, we worked with these executives to improve all six benchmarks though particularly honing in on the three identified areas of weakness. One executive was released to "free agency" since he refused to improve his own corporate character (visits to various "gentlemen's clubs" was no longer going to be tolerated). Attunement was the hardest aspect for this executive team, but they worked faithfully at creating more unity for the good of everyone involved.

At the end of the second year, there was an overwhelming increase in positive feelings toward the executive team and a spike in general employee satisfaction, as shown in an Employee Satisfaction Survey. This positive trend has continued every year since our work began. Annual net profits have also continued to rise. The corporate family as a whole is healthy, happy, and profitable, and we trust that the individual families of these executives would report just about the same results.

Although most leaders won't become a legend like John D. Rockefeller, you can strive toward improving your performance by intentionally implementing the Six Benchmarks for Internal and Intentional Leadership. As you do so, you'll positively impact those around you, and you will be more prepared than ever to meet the challenges that you're bound to face in the journey ahead.

SHARPENING YOUR EDGE

1. Review the list of Benchmarks for Internal and Intentional Leadership.

   Initiate

   Communicate

   Motivate

   Sustain

   Create Commonality of Purpose

   Exhibit Corporate Character

   Highlight the benchmarks that you feel are your greatest strengths. Put a delta sign by any benchmark where you need improvement. If you are serious about sharpening your edge, ask a small group in your professional life—superiors, peers, and subordinates—how they would rate you against your benchmarks.

2. Write some short-term goals relating to any benchmark that is below standard. Announce these goals to those in your sphere of influence, and tell them how you plan to improve over the next month. We recommend a mentor/protégée relationship for optimum growth.

3. How would people in your personal life rate you when it comes to Hall of Fame Leadership and these Six Benchmarks for Internal and Intentional Leadership?

4. Is there any significant area where alignment needs to occur? How attuned is your team? What plan needs to be developed in order to ensure the alignment and attunement of your team?

5. If you are leading a team and you identify weaknesses in a particular benchmark, then establish a game plan for all team members to have the same opportunity for transformation as you do.

Discovering Personal and Professional Life Balance*

*Some people think that the higher up you are in a corpora-
tion the more you have to neglect your family. Not at all!
Actually it's the guys at the top who have the freedom and
flexibility to spend enough time with their wives and kids.*
Lee Iacocca, former CEO of Chrysler

M ike Johnson's seventy-plus hour work week was just
the beginning of his problems when he entered our
offices at the end of a particularly grueling year for his company. Demands from an overly-controlling CEO, stock-
holder dissatisfaction, and union troubles all added pressure
to this COO's professional life. After an hour-long conference with Mike, we also discovered that his twenty-two year
marriage was struggling, he rarely spent time with his three

---

*We greatly appreciate the assistance of Dr. Ron Jenson whose book,
Achieving Authentic Success: 10 Timeless Life Principles That Will Maximize
Your Real Potential (2006), is the foundation for many of the concepts we
will share with you in this chapter.

kids, and he was overweight due to terrible eating patterns and lack of exercise. Also, his physician had just added a high blood pressure medication to his regimen of pills.

In short, Mike was a personal and professional mess. He dreaded going to work, but he felt that his job was a diversion from his unhappy home life. He worked late to avoid the inevitable conflict he'd face when he did eventually return home and to ensure he'd receive a larger bonus than he had the previous year. Because he'd been on the fast track since graduating college, Mike believed that his six-figure salary, large corner office, and house in an exclusive neighborhood represented his success. But this savvy businessman was anything but satisfied with his life. If he had a mentor like Lee Iacocca, Mike might have avoided some of the negative circumstances he was experiencing, and he would have been able to understand that life balance is not just about surviving but truly about thriving!

> Life balance is not just about surviving but truly about thriving!

Mike's story is distressing and unfortunately all too common among the leaders we speak with. Somehow they've bought into the misconception that the harder they work, the more successful and satisfied they'll be. The names change, and the degree of imbalance varies, but all of these leaders are stretched to the max. They continually squeeze just one more thing into their jammed schedules, believing that then they'll finally be a terrific leader. But as author Henri Nouwen observed, "Our lives and schedules are filled full and we feel unfulfilled."

> "Our lives and schedules are filled full and we feel unfulfilled."

Perhaps you can relate to Mike's dilemma. Maybe you're struggling to keep up with an out-of-control schedule, cutting back on sleep so that you can fit in a few more things each day. You might understand his dread of going to the office, yet needing to fill the hours in the day because you wouldn't want to be home anyway. Could it be that you've spent so much time on the treadmill of professional success that you haven't seen a treadmill, bike trail, or gym in months?

If any of these scenarios describe you, we're here to tell you that you are living on an extremely dangerous edge—and not the leading edge of success! Eventually this type of high-powered living will result in a personal and professional downward spiral.

Hopefully your life is nowhere near this level of chaos, but we're going to show you how to avoid these types of problems and pitfalls. Personal and professional balance is integral to improving your performance—and to attaining and maintaining the leading edge throughout your entire life.

> Personal and professional balance is integral to improving your performance—and to attaining and maintaining the leading edge throughout your entire life.

In the past few chapters, we've shown that your professional life will be impacted by your personal one, and vice-versa. This concept may be a new one to you; after all, life balance is rarely discussed in business courses, internship programs, or evaluation meetings. In fact, after an exhaustive search of leadership development resources, we found few or no references to the critical nature of balance in leaders' lives. We noticed that "organization health" was mentioned several times, but rarely was personal health discussed (Lencioni, 2000; Blayney, 2006; Dive, 2004).

That's not to say that we don't strongly believe that organizational health is important, but what would a business be without healthy individuals running it? According to Drs. Ron Loeppke and Wayne Burton (2003), productivity decreases as the number of employee health risks increase. When leaders are stressed, over-worked, or going through personal crises, it affects the company's overall performance, productivity, and profitability.

> Leaders must understand that individual and corporate health go hand-in-hand.

T. Boone Pickens, chairman of BP Capital Management and one of the wealthiest men in America, believed so strongly in the impact of individual health on the corporation that he spent $2.5 million to build a fitness center at Mesa Petroleum in Amarillo, Texas. In addition, he instituted a wellness program so that the workforce would have more opportunity to improve its health. Everyone benefited, and the productivity and profitability of the corporation increased (Pickens, 2008).

This doesn't mean you need to build your own gym, start a corporate nutrition program, or co-op with a mental health center in order to keep your corporate family fit. However, leaders must understand that individual and corporate health go hand-in-hand. It's up to you to spearhead the efforts to keep your organization and teams balanced and in good shape!

MAXIMIZING YOUR ABILITY TO DISCOVER LIFE BALANCE

We believe that personal and professional balance is the cornerstone of your success. Balance is good for business, and it's even better for you. Ignoring this straight line and allowing part of your life to be unbalanced will impact the bottom line. However, if you put the following principles into practice, you will not only experience more productivity and profitability, but also overall success. Conversely, lack of attention to your well-being—whether physical, mental, spiritual, or emotional—will have its own set of consequences: decreased productivity, profitability, and significance, especially in terms of long-term legacy.

> Balance is good for business, and it's even better for you.

Let's begin with the ten top principles, or MAXIMIZERS (Jenson, 2006):

Make Things Happen

Achieve Personal Significance

X-Out the Negatives

Internalize Right Principles

March to a Mission

Integrate All of Life

Zero in on Caring for People

Energize Internally

Realign Rigorously

Stay the Course

Leaders who **make things happen** take charge of all aspects of their lives. They don't wait around for something or someone to magically appear. Instead, they are proactive, *intentional* leaders who are invested in **achieving personal significance** and fulfilling their own sense of destiny. Rather than needing others to encourage or give them kudos, these men and women know they have a purpose in life, and they work to do everything possible to fulfill that destiny. Taking time to think about how you view your own sense of significance is important as you begin this leadership development process.

> Rather than needing others to encourage or give them kudos, these men and women know they have a purpose in life, and they work to do everything possible to fulfill that destiny.

X-ing out negatives is another essential step in the journey toward exceptional leadership. All leaders will be faced with less than ideal circumstances throughout their lives, but the ability to find the positive, especially in the midst of challenge, increases performance. We're confident that you could easily compile a list of negatives you've had to deal with this year alone. Consider how you could have handled these if you'd viewed them more as "opportunities" as opposed to negative experiences.

> Consider how you could have handled these if you'd viewed them more as "opportunities" as opposed to negative experiences.

Having a personal and professional life based on solid values and beliefs also impacts your ultimate productivity. By **internalizing right principles,** you will always have guidelines (or "straight lines") to help your decision-making process. Think about what you truly value. What beliefs do you hold that help you make decisions each day?

Outstanding leaders definitely **march to a mission**, and establishing that mission is a personal choice. What do you want to accomplish when it's all said and done? How are you going to get there—actively, routinely, and *intentionally?* As you seek to fulfill your mission, you should **integrate all aspects of living**. This is the heart of that life balance we're emphasizing. That doesn't mean that everything has to be perfect in your life (not only would that be too much pressure, but it's also unattainable). Instead, balancing involves regularly checking, re-working, and re-booting everything from personal to corporate health. In a sense, you're in a state of constant cross-training, just like an athlete, in order to stay in peak condition for your "sport." How can you do a better job of cross-training your personal and professional life?

> Men and women are relationship-oriented, so leaders must connect with their colleagues and subordinates in a caring, compassionate manner.

Zeroing in on caring for others often seems too "warm and fuzzy" for some leaders, especially in the workplace. But people are people whether at home, at a ball-game, at church or synagogue, at a party, or at the office. Men and women are relationship-oriented, so leaders must connect with their colleagues and subordinates in a caring, compassionate manner. Legendary college football coach Lou Holtz sums this concept up succinctly: "When you concern yourself with the welfare of others, you engender loyalty and respect. You create value. And you acquire power" (2005, p. 181). The capacity to truly care about others is enhanced when you improve your EQ skill sets (Chapter 2). Consider ways you can show more concern for the people in your life, and then try a few of these ideas out over the next several weeks. We're confident this caring approach will pay off in multiple ways.

The concept of **energizing internally** involves cultivating character and behavior that are at the highest personal and professional standards. The development of your character is critical because it is your source of strength, particularly when things get tough. What do people around you think about your character? Do your behavior patterns and daily actions reflect your choices about good morals and values? Exceptional leaders also learn how to **rigorously realign** when things get out of balance. Throughout our lives, obstacles pop up, usually at the most inconvenient times; positively adjusting to these obstructions allows you to stay flexible and moving in a forward direction.

> Finding the leading edge in your personal and professional life must entail keeping your eyes focused on the finish line—no matter what.

Finally, none of these MAXIMIZERS will serve you in the long run without *internally* and *intentionally* exercising your determination to **stay the course**. Finding the leading edge in your personal and professional life must entail keeping your eyes focused on the finish line—no matter what. What do you see your family looking like at the end of life's journey? What will your circle of friends look like when you eventually retire? How do you envision your business and corporate family carrying on when you hand over control someday? (We'll discuss much more about legacy in Chapter 10).

> "When I slow down, I go faster"

LEADERSHIP BEGINS WITH YOU

For some leaders, even taking the time to think about these kinds of issues seems wasteful. A few have told us, "I've got to worry about how we're going to meet our goals this month," or "There's too much happening right now—I'll deal with these issues when I've got more time." You know as well as we do that, with this attitude, there will always be too much going on! While it may seem counter-intuitive, reflection and re-adjustment will allow you to become *more productive* in the long run. Ken Blanchard reminds all of us that, "When I slow down, I go faster" (1995, p. 44).

> You're the one who must lead. You have control over your situation at work, at home, and everywhere in between.

All too often leaders focus only on their technical skills and intellectual capabilities, never taking time to look at the bigger picture of what makes them "tick." As Albert Einstein explained, "We should take care not to make intellect our god. It has, of course, powerful muscles, but no personality. It cannot lead, it can only serve." You're the one who must lead. You have control over your situation at work, at home, and everywhere in between. You have the power to

> "Good leadership begins with self-leadership."

improve your personal and professional circumstances, even if they are far from perfect. And now you have some powerful principles to make these important changes. As our colleague Dr. Jenson states, "Good leadership begins with self-leadership."

Another way of looking at life balance involves the seven "F's":

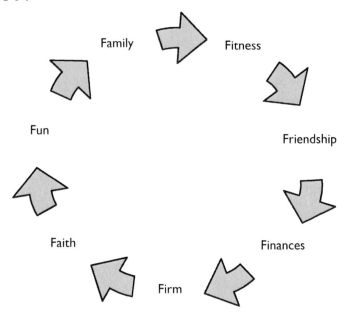

These are the seven basic areas that comprise life. Notice that "Firm," meaning your career and corporate life, is only one fraction of the entire picture. If you have been heavily focused on this one area, it's no surprise that other parts of your life are out of whack. Take some time right now to evaluate how you're doing in each of these areas. Come up with some specific strategies on how you can begin to strengthen those weak aspects of your life. Eliminate some of the "busyness" in your schedule so you can intentionally make improvements in these critical components to life balance.

Of course, leaders can find a measure of success without equalizing these factors; in fact, there are many examples of powerful leaders who've accomplished a great deal—even impacting cities, nations, and the world at large—whose personal and professional lives have not always been in balance. But, we're convinced no leader will attain the ultimate level of success and significance he or she is seeking without bringing these into a state of equilibrium.

Margaret Thatcher, former Prime Minister of England, is one example of imbalance affecting leadership. She worked her way up the political ladder and helped shape the Western World in the late 20th century, yet historians have noted that many of her weaknesses came directly from her strengths. "She sought to control everything, rarely delegated authority, slept for only four hours a night... her self-confidence slid easily into intolerance, inflexibility, and moralism...she was famous for insulting individuals gratuitously" (Gardner & Laskin, 1995, p. 238).

> But, we're convinced no leader will attain the ultimate level of success and significance he or she is seeking without bringing these into a state of equilibrium.

While Thatcher's accomplishments are admirable, her term in office was not pleasant for her or those around her. According to Gardner & Laskin's research, "She was widely seen, even by supporters, as domineering, mean-spirited, divisive, and unbending. On television, she appeared as 'bossy' to many members of the general public" (1995, p. 238). You may have known people like this. Perhaps former leaders or executive "role models" might have exemplified some of the same traits. Did you ever stop to wonder what their personal lives were like? If they treated co-workers and subordinates in unkind, uncompassionate ways, how did family and friends feel when they were around them?

If these thoughts are hitting a little too close to home, then you've even more reason to spend time reflecting on how out-of-balance your life may actually be. Are you, like Thatcher, trying to survive on four hours of sleep a night? If so, sleep-deprivation is a likely cause of any irritability and short-temperedness during your waking twenty hours. Consider your diet and the kind of exercise routine you are maintaining—or ignoring. Think about the last time you did something fun, and just for you. Do you make enjoying your family and friends a priority, or do you pass that off as something to work on "when you have more time?" Are you developing your mental and spiritual well-being, or do your only plans for self-improvement involve attending another conference or completing hours for some new certification?

MIKE FINALLY FINDS BALANCE

If you're thinking that these kinds of changes are next to impossible given your current situation, maybe we can encourage you by telling you the rest of Mike Johnson's story. As we mentioned, Mike's life was nearly in shambles when we first met him. But Mike had one of the key ingredients necessary for exceptional leadership: he was firmly committed to "staying the course"—that "S" in MAXIMIZERS. He'd never been a quitter, and he made it very clear to all of us at LEADon that he didn't ever intend to be one.

During our initial meetings with Mike, we noted that he had several other MAXIMIZERS principles in place, including great character (Internalize Right Principles) and the ability to be proactive (Make Things Happen). Mike had struggled with keeping all aspects of his life in balance and realigning when obstacles crossed his path.

Once Mike spent time getting some personal coaching on the missing leadership principles, he began to adjust his approach to life and his unbalanced schedule. In addition to a visit to his doctor to coordinate a healthy weight-loss plan, he renewed a gym membership and added some personal training to jump start the process. Although this workout schedule meant heading to the gym at five in the morning instead of his favorite coffee shop, Mike quickly discovered that the increase in exercise replaced his former craving for caffeine.

We wish we could report that all of Mike's seven "F's" were adjusted this quickly and effectively. Unfortunately, even after trying marriage counseling, Mike and his wife divorced. The good news is that the couple did so amicably for the sake of their three children, and now Mike is rebuilding the relationships with his kids that he'd placed on the back burner for years. While still strongly committed to his firm, Mike has realized that his career is just a slice of his life and taking care of his physical, mental, spiritual, and emotional well-being improved his job performance and his sense of significance.

> While you may have many of these life balance principles in place, if you don't intentionally work to maintain them, then they could quickly get out of alignment, too.

We hope you will uncover the same truth that Mike found. While you may have many of these life balance principles in place, if you don't intentionally work to maintain them, then they could quickly get out of alignment, too. The balance beam for exceptional leadership is a narrow one, but if you master these skills, you'll glide across yours just like an Olympic gymnast. All you need is practice—and lots of it!

SHARPENING YOUR EDGE

1. Which of the seven "F's" are your greatest strengths? In which of these seven do you need significant improvement? Write specific goals, including a time frame, that will improve areas of greatest need.

2. Evaluate the overall health of your team and/or "Sphere of Influence." Meet with them and have them evaluate themselves in light of the seven "F's." Brainstorm ways in which individually and as a group you can improve the balance of your personal and professional lives in order to keep your edge sharp!

3. Now repeat #2 using the ten MAXIMIZERS principles as your focus.

4. Face-time and fun are absolute virtues for the corporate family. Do you have parties, picnics, family fun nights, or other activities as part of your regular schedule?

Part II

3 PROFESSIONAL STRATEGIES

Fielding Your
High Performance Team

Where there is no vision, the people perish.

Hebrew Proverb

The past chapters have specifically dealt with you, the leader, and the multifaceted aspects of who you are and who you can become. As we transition into Part II, Professional Strategies, we want to remind you that you are merely shifting gears, not lanes, on the road to exceptional leadership. In other words, the personal approaches we've discussed in Part I *must* consistently be implemented by you in the days ahead, but you will be adding new strategies to your game plan that will focus directly on the professional aspects of your life.

Although many of us tend to compartmentalize life, most aspects of leadership transcend a specific time or place. For instance, good parenting at home requires EQ skills (Chapter 2), the ability to communicate (Chapter 3), and a healthy balance in your personal and professional life (Chapter 4). Likewise, many of your best parenting skills will help you in your daily interactions with subordinates. In fact, you may feel like you're doing more parenting at work than at home some days.

> Personal approaches must consistently be implemented by you in the days ahead, but you will be adding new strategies to your game plan that will focus directly on the professional aspects of your life.

Whether you lead two or two thousand people, the personal strategies you've been honing will serve you well. After all, people are people no matter the venue. There are, however, specific tactics that are necessary to improve your professional abilities, including being able to field, develop, and maintain High Performance Teams (HPTs). Despite the complex, "blended family" issues that may exist in your organization, you can learn how to break down barriers and get everyone in your company working cooperatively instead of competitively. You can build a team in which everyone enjoys working together and is passionate about accomplishing your business plan.

This chapter focuses specifically on fielding that kind of team; then, we will assist you in some "straight line" strategies necessary to develop and maintain that team in Chapters 6 and 7. While all aspects of High Performance Teams are important for leaders to understand, the health of those teams is critical for ultimate success. This process of fielding a stable HPT is the foundation upon which everything else in your leadership plan must be built. You would never dream of constructing a house without firm footings and a stable foundation. Likewise, your company might be shaky because there's nothing high performance about any of your teams. To change that, we'll begin by looking at five specific strategies that will prepare you to field the HPT you've been looking for:

HPT

Placing
Right People
in Right Roles

Developing the
Organizational Chart

Discovering Your
Leadership Style

Establishing the Mission

Setting the Vision

STRATEGY #1: SETTING THE VISION

Decades ago, if a leader brought up the term vision, he or she might be laughed right out of the board room. Business models back in the day involved what people considered hard sell, hard science, and hard currency. Today leaders have come to realize that picturing the direction their organizations should take, envisioning how to reach the goals of the business plan, and attempting to anticipate future developments are essential to overall success.

The Hebrew proverb above was penned thousands of years before our time, and its truth has stood the test of time. Vision empowers and provides a clear path for people; lack of vision weakens and causes men and women to struggle and stumble. Many leaders throughout history have grasped this concept and attempted to pass along their vision, knowing full well it may not be welcomed or accepted by everyone. In fact, John F. Kennedy quoted this proverb on the eve of his assassination (Sorenson, 1996).

> Today leaders have come to realize that picturing the direction their organizations should take, envisioning how to reach the goals of the business plan, and attempting to anticipate future developments are essential to overall success.

Not everyone will like the vision, but that does not preclude the necessity for exceptional leaders to proclaim it anyway. But how can you begin to grasp the vision for yourself, your HPT, and your company? According to Goleman, Boyatzis, & McKee, "to connect with the kind of vision that can move a culture toward resonance, emotionally intelligent leaders start by looking inside—at what they feel, think, and sense about their organizations" (1996, p. 205). These experts also admit this process requires leaders to take time to reflect on their own dreams as well as the overall aspirations of the organization's stakeholders.

> Not everyone will like the vision, but that does not preclude the necessity for exceptional leaders to proclaim it anyway.

Have you asked yourself lately why you are even in your business? Think about what you hope to achieve, where you would like to see the company in the next five or ten years. Consider which people and processes are currently in place to get your business there as well as what might not be beneficial to this overall vision. Have you enlisted the assistance of your colleagues and subordinates to clarify that vision? "Side by side with the rest of the organization, leaders co-create the vision that will serve to rally and energize the group as a whole" (Goleman, Boyatzis, & McKee, 2002, p. 206).

If you haven't thought about your vision for some time, then this is a critical first step as you start the process of improving your professional skills. Many leadership development experts recommend that leaders take time to retreat on occasion to set a vision. If you can't get away for a day or two, then take a few hours, find a quiet place, and think about your dreams, hopes and aspirations, for you and for your company. Some men and women simply close their office doors, turn their electronic equipment off (yes, even the Blackberry!), and spend time writing their thoughts. We recommend that you leave the workplace environment and take a long walk or go to a park, lake, or beach. Clear your mind of all other matters except for the vision. If you think you'll forget some of those ideas, then bring along a pad and pen; jot some notes so you can reflect on these thoughts when you do return to the office. Wherever this process takes place, when it comes to setting the vision, the best advice we can offer is simple: *just do it!*

STRATEGY #2: ESTABLISHING THE MISSION

After you have the chance to get the big picture, or vision, then it's time to establish the mission. By definition, the word mission refers to a specific task or purpose. Collins and Porras describe it as "the organization's fundamental reasons for existence beyond just making money—a perpetual guiding star on the horizon" (1997, p. 73).

This mission is buoyed by the core values of the organization, including the values, beliefs, and behavior patterns that help to define the company.

This mission is buoyed by the core values of the organization, including the values, beliefs, and behavior patterns that help to define the company. (We'll talk more about these three pillars to your Corporate Culture in Chapter 9.) Values are "a small set of general guiding principles, not to be confused with specific cultural or operating practices" (Collins & Porras, 1997, p. 73). In other words, they represent the basic philosophy of your organization that will *never* be compromised— even if times get tough, if the economy struggles, or if other businesses are cheating in order to get ahead.

Many companies today have established a simple mission statement that summarizes their overall purpose. This typically is a brief statement about the reason an organization is in business, beyond the financial aspect. For instance, a San Diego-based, non-profit organization posts the following statement on its website: "The mission of the Alpha Project is to empower individuals, families, and communities by providing work, recovery, and support services to people who are motivated to change their lives and achieve self-sufficiency" (www.alphaproject.org). Their purpose is clearly defined, straightforward, and serves as a "guiding star" for all employees.

As a leader, you must help your organization find that guide and be certain that every member of your corporate family is aware of the overall mission. Often we assume that men and women who form new companies are the luckiest individuals, having the opportunity to establish the mission statement and core values from the ground up. But starting without any "North Star" for guidance isn't easy for those leaders. On the other hand, many executives inherit the responsibility of continuing an established mission, but sometimes the heart of the mission has been lost or changed after being in existence for so long.

Your mission statement must reflect your current values, beliefs and behavior patterns. If it doesn't, then you and your HPT need to re-visit and revise it so that the mission statement truly expresses what the corporate family stands for and strives to achieve.

Exceptional leadership also involves rallying the troops to commit to the mission for the good of everyone involved, especially stakeholders. As a leader, you need to be the first to firmly commit to the mission of your organization. Those who want to attain the leading edge "have genuine passion for their mission, and that passion is contagious. Their enthusiasm and excitement spread spontaneously, invigorating those they lead" (Goleman, Boyatzis & McKee, 2002, p. 248).

> Your mission statement must reflect your current values, beliefs and behavior patterns.

In addition, the core values you and your corporate family establish must support this mission. Three to six core values are typically sufficient, and each should be "simple, clear, straightforward, and powerful" (Collins & Porras, 1997, p. 74). If your organization tries to put too many in place, it may mean that you haven't pared things down to the real core of what you value and believe. For example, one core value at a food company might be "Only the best quality will be produced and sold to our customer," while a retail business may state "Customers are our first priority." Choose the values that are most important to your company and hold to them no matter what.

Whether you are in a start-up company or leading a well-established organization, ensuring that a sound mission statement and set of core values are in place must be among your first priorities before you can truly develop High Performance Teams. Once you accomplish this, you will discover that you, your corporate family members, and your business will be able to run at peak levels of performance.

STRATEGY #3: DISCOVERING YOUR LEADERSHIP STYLE

Although most leaders are keenly aware of the importance of their roles, many that we meet have seldom analyzed the style in which they operate daily. How you choose to lead is often determined by what was role-modeled to you during your formative years as well as throughout your educational and vocational experiences. At one time people assumed there were two basic leadership styles: *autocratic* and *democratic* (Blanchard, 1985). Autocratic leaders were the tough guys who were typically domineering and controlling in any and every area related to their companies.

> How you choose to lead is often determined by what was role-modeled to you during your formative years as well as throughout your educational and vocational experiences.

Although those who led more democratically were viewed as more open and friendly, they were also often seen as soft and far too easy-going. In the past few decades, we've discovered that there are several styles in which leaders operate.

According to Goleman, Boyatzis, & McKee, "the most effective leaders act according to one or more of six distinct approaches to leadership and skillfully switch between the various styles depending on the situation" (2002, p. 53). Blanchard (1985), while differing slightly on his classifications for these styles, agrees that exceptional leaders must be able to utilize many approaches as well as flexibly navigate between them depending on the needs that arise throughout the day.

SIX STYLES OF LEADERSHIP

Visionary
Coaching
Affiliative
Democratic
Pacesetting
Commanding

We're going to start with the first four styles because they offer the opportunity to be the most productive in your work with people. The last two are slightly more challenging, or, perhaps better put, they are "useful in some very specific situations [and] should be applied with caution" (Goleman, Boyatzis, & McKee, 2002, p. 53).

Visionary leaders move others toward shared dreams. As we discussed earlier, human beings need a vision or they tend to struggle. Obviously, all leaders must be able to inspire others to see the big picture and follow that image as they journey together in corporate life, but if you are a visionary leader, realize that you don't need to set a vision each and every day. Sometimes the original vision-setting

> Visionary leaders move others toward shared dreams.

will be enough to sustain your company through many seasons until such a time arises that a new direction or emphasis may be required.

Leaders who use *coaching* techniques connect with others, evaluate their needs and desires, and consider how they see the organization's goals advancing. When you think about a coach, you probably envision someone on the sidelines who gives direction, listens to feedback, then provides the guidance and inspiration necessary to get the job done. Many people (including those outside of athletics) flourish when coached in the right direction.

> Many people (including those outside of athletics) flourish when coached in the right direction.

Affiliative leadership creates a sense of harmony and connection between individuals. These leaders are relationship builders, and they realize that the better their teams are at conflict resolution, the more chances the corporate family has of achieving the business goals. During the most stressful seasons, affiliative leaders rise to the challenge, improving communication and repairing broken trust among co-workers.

> During the most stressful seasons, affiliative leaders rise to the challenge, improving communication and repairing broken trust among co-workers.

The new version of the *democratic leader* is someone who values people's input and is able to get buy-in from corporate family members. These individuals have a strong sense that ideas gleaned from the employees will enhance the decision-making process, and they are willing to accept the bad news about the company as well as the good when they undertake information-gathering.

However, democratic leaders must be careful not to over-rely on this process because it can also exasperate employees rather than inspire enthusiasm.

As we mentioned, *pacesetting* and *commanding leadership styles* must be used with caution because they can negatively affect climate and performance (Fullan, 2001). Many leaders thrive under pacesetting formats; they set high standards of performance and demand a lot of themselves. These individuals also flourish with challenging and exciting goals. The problem is other employees may not work this way or this well. Moreover, pacesetters are quick to pinpoint poor performers, demanding more and more from them, then rescuing the situation when these employees don't rise to the occasion, completely defeating already demoralized workers. Therefore, this method is best implemented when a highly competent team is in place (we will discuss how to ensure this in Strategies #4 and #5).

The same care must be applied to the commanding style, or what would have been termed autocratic in the past. This, "do it because I say so," methodology is best utilized in times of crisis or when a clear direction must be implemented quickly and efficiently for the good of the organization. For example, during the 2008—2009 economic crisis, many leaders simply had to take hold of the reigns and make drastic changes in order to help their companies survive. In times like those, employees' fears are alleviated, but a constant implementation of this style eventually creates resentment among workers who feel that their opinions don't matter to their organization.

As you analyze these varying styles of leadership, work on improving those skill sets that you already have in place and develop any that you've noted are areas of weakness. There are numerous resources available to assist you in this process (see some we've sourced above), and don't be afraid to seek the assistance of a leadership development expert or other mentor.

STRATEGY #4: DEVELOPING YOUR ORGANIZATIONAL CHART

You may be wondering why so much of this chapter has been focused on you when we are to be discussing how to field High Performance Teams. If that's what you're thinking, then you have definitely gotten our message:

1. Fielding a High Performance Team must begin with you, the exceptional leader.
2. As a leader, you are responsible for ensuring that the vision is set, the mission is established, and your leadership style is being perfected for the good of the entire corporate family.

> Fielding a High Performance Team must begin with you, the exceptional leader. As a leader, you are responsible for ensuring that the vision is set, the mission is established, and your leadership style is being perfected for the good of the entire corporate family.

Once these important strategies are in place then—and only then—will you be able to successfully navigate the next part of the journey toward getting that HPT in place.

Developing your organizational chart may not be the most exciting work that you've ever done, but it certainly will be one of the most rewarding in terms of success and significance for you and your organization. And while understanding current employee roles is vital, *knowing what they should be* is the most essential aspect of this strategy. Too few people on your organizational chart can be problematic; keeping too many employees is simply bad for business.

Completing a detailed analysis of your company's organizational chart may result in a brutal reality check, including discovering that you may have the wrong staff or the wrong players in certain positions, and even wrong expectations for both. While this may hurt your pride or even challenge you with some unpleasant responsibilities (letting people go to get the right individuals in place), exceptional leaders are willing to move outside their comfort zones for the overall good of the corporate family. "One of the dominant themes from our research is that breakthrough results come by a series of good decisions, diligently executed and accumulated one on top of another" (Collins, 2001, p. 69).

> Developing your organizational chart may not be the most exciting work that you've ever done, but it certainly will be one of the most rewarding in terms of success and significance for you and your organization.

This good-decision making can start today. It doesn't matter what problems exist or what choices you made in the past. Today is what counts, and tomorrow can only get better if you're willing to make sound decisions, one right after the other. Start by identifying all of the roles that must be filled (we will discuss how to find the right people for those roles in Strategy #5). All of these positions must be filled with key players to meet the objectives of your business plan. If you don't need six people in marketing, then adjust the situation. If

> Today is what counts, and tomorrow can only get better if you're willing to make sound decisions, one right after the other.

fifty employees in the field aren't enough to accomplish the work, make the changes necessary to allow room for more and improve the success of your company.

As you study your current organizational chart and begin to strategize about the new and improved model, start thinking about the standards that should be in place for each of these positions. *With specific roles come respective responsibilities, which must be clearly defined from the beginning.* Remember the chaos that we discovered at Bantham Industrial Supplies in Chapter 1? Much of the mess revolved around a disastrous organizational chart where the roles were unclear and those who filled them lacked accountability for their responsibilities to the business plan. The standards or "straight lines" you establish now for these positions will set the bar for all current and future corporate family members.

> With specific roles come respective responsibilities, which must be clearly defined from the beginning.

Fielding a company with position players who understand their roles and responsibilities is how the best organizations function. While this process is not the only component necessary to fielding a High Performance Team, "structure does make a difference" (Fullan, 2001, p. 43). So, reflect on what you've got, re-design, re-organize according to what you need, and get ready to experience some dramatic changes as you start filing those positions with the right people.

> Fielding a company with position players who understand their roles and responsibilities is how the best organizations function.

STRATEGY #5: PLACING THE RIGHT PEOPLE IN THE RIGHT ROLES AND RESPONSIBILITIES

We're finally at the core of fielding your High Performance Team. Your organizational chart is in shape, so now what? As a leader, you must be certain that each and every role has a "position player" just like those on a baseball, basketball, soccer, or football team. Can you imagine a football team with a kicker who wanted to be the quarterback? Games would be disastrous if the coach allowed it, say because he'd been doing the job (though badly) for months or even years, or worse, the kicker was a relative. Maybe the coach simply didn't think he'd find anyone else who wanted to fill the position, so he let the kicker stay in there, even though the team lost game after game. In the world of sports, this just wouldn't happen with winning teams—at least not for very long. So why do we allow the same situations to occur in our corporate families?

Get the "kicker" (i.e., whoever is out of position on your organizational chart) into a place where he or she can utilize his or her skill sets for the good of everyone involved. From the receptionist to the CEO, customer support to the president, every person must fulfill a specific role that is vital to the success of the business plan. And *everyone* on the payroll must exhibit the Hall of Fame attributes discussed in Chapter 2. Every existing and future leader must aspire to the Six Benchmarks for Internal and Intentional Leadership (Chapter 3), and Personal and Professional Life Balance (Chapter 4) must be part of the foundation that all corporate family members, including you, strive to attain.

The process of finding the right people for the right roles and responsibilities is both *internal* and *intentional*. Once you've repositioned current players, recruiting will become a big part of getting other key individuals you need. As a leader, it will be crucial that you find men and women who best meet the demands each role on your organizational chart requires so that your company can compete in the marketplace, and better yet, win! Because of this, we encourage leaders to seek out "Blue Ribbon Players" only. In other words, your first objective should be to search for those individuals who have a "winner take all" mindset. Those who are satisfied with red, yellow, or green ribbons need not apply at your company. Why? Because you're playing for profits, not self-esteem. Your success and significance and that of your organization depend on your determination to find the *best and brightest* to complete your organizational chart.

> The process of finding the right people for the right roles and responsibilities is both internal and intentional.

Former producer for ABC Radio, management consultant, and author Laurence Haughton explains that "a number of successful leaders and managers feel that hiring for the right attitudes assures a much better fit than hiring for the right experience" (2004, p. 56). Some of these attitudes include agility in learning new concepts, the ability to deal with ambiguity, good EQ skills, self-motivation, and self-sufficiency. As we've stated before, no one should be in an interview with you who doesn't have an exemplary resume; that should have been the ticket for

> The test these potential employees must pass is to be able to communicate to you how they will fit into the overall expectations and culture of your corporate family.

admission. The test these potential employees must pass is to be able to communicate to you how they will fit into the overall expectations and culture of your corporate family.

Haughton also encourages leaders to seek out those "champions" who are empathetic; in other words, individuals who have "the ability to recognize feelings, thoughts, and experiences of another without necessarily having those feelings... themselves" (2004, p. 91). This brings us to the topic of gender. Many studies have been done on women's natural ability to care and be compassionate, and this can certainly impact the workplace—including management—for the better. In fact, according to a *Time* article "there is growing evidence that in today's marketplace the female management style is not only distinctly different but also essential" (Shipman & Kay, 5/20/09).

Thankfully we have seen a marked increase in the number of women in leadership roles in numerous industries. In addition to their technical skills, leaders need to be aware of the impact women can have on the overall business goals and objectives. This *Time* article also reported that 83% of all consumer purchases are controlled by women. If your company needs to improve its EQ abilities as well as its understanding of females in the marketplace, then perhaps you need to be recruiting more women for roles within your organization, especially positions of leadership.

> **Finally, remember that people are personal—not personnel.**

Finally, remember that people are personal—not personnel. As you reorganize your company and recruit new members to your corporate family, don't just look for a body to fill a chair, but a person that fulfills needs and complements the members of your High Performance Team. On a planet of six billion people, the right ones are out there somewhere; as a leader, it's your job to take the time and effort to find them!

AN EXPERT IN FIELDING A HPT

Six months before we met him, Bob Jenkins had contacted a firm across town to provide graphic arts services for his retail company. Bob was immediately impressed by the friendliness of the receptionist who took his call and spent time asking him a series of informational questions for her boss, Sydney Lindstrom. After speaking to Sydney later that day, a contract was issued and Bob's dilemma about finding the right graphic arts specialist was resolved.

Bob shared with us that he stopped by Designer Graphics the next week to take a look at some materials they were working on, and again he noticed the professionalism of the receptionist, Anisha Jones. She greeted Bob with a smile and talked to him about his business while they waited for Sydney to finish up with another client. Bob couldn't help but think about the rather cranky receptionist who answered the phones at his company; Mindy tended to ruffle people's feathers, but Anisha soothed them. In fact, Mindy was often involved in the inner-office conflicts that had been springing up with more regularity.

After their meeting, Sydney gave Bob a tour of her small firm's facilities. She talked to him about the cohesive group she'd been hired to lead five years ago, their company spirit, and the great environment that everyone worked to maintain. Bob noticed a poster with core values posted in the lobby as well as the company slogan on T-shirts worn by several employees they spoke with during the tour.

"I like your slogan, 'You define it, we design it'–it's catchy," Bob commented as he prepared to leave.

"Thank you," Sydney replied, "It's a shortened version of the mission statement that we all decided on. And, since we're a graphic arts business, it was pretty easy to design our own

T-shirts! I believe this company has the potential to become a leader in our industry one day."

On his way back to the office, Bob thought about the great work environment at Designer Graphics, and as he pulled into his parking spot, he realized at that moment he wished he could be back there rather than preparing to walk into his own building. That feeling was part of what prompted Bob to contact LEADon.

Interestingly enough, Bob shared with us that he still calls Designer Graphics from time to time, even though he hasn't needed their services for a few months. Part of the reason is that he simply enjoys the friendly way Anisha answers the phone.

"On really bad days around here, I call Anisha. She lifts my mood by talking to her. I wouldn't get that feeling by talking to Mindy."

What Bob experienced is the nutshell of what we've been discussing. Sydney Lindstrom had implemented many of the strategies for fielding a High Performance Team. She had a vision, a mission, and was comfortable in her leadership style. From what Bob told us, the right people were in the right positions, starting with the point person: the receptionist. And the corporate culture at Designer Graphics was so comfortable that even Bob wanted to stay—or at least call the business occasionally to stay connected to it.

As you process these strategies over the coming days and weeks, please remember that no one expects you to become an expert in them overnight. Fielding a High Performance Team should take time; rushing the process will only create more problems. We hope the main concept you've gotten is the big picture about the vision for your organization. We're going to continue helping you along this journey toward exceptional leadership, especially now that you're beginning to put that HPT in place.

SHARPENING YOUR EDGE

1. Have you shared your vision for the company with your corporate family members? Do your HPT members believe in that vision? Do they own it, and have they made it their own?

2. Does your corporate family have a mission statement? Does it reflect your current values, beliefs, and behavior patterns? Is your vision and/or mission statement publically displayed? Finally, what mechanism for accountability to the vision and mission statement do you have in place for corporate family members?

3. Pinpoint your key leadership style from Strategy #3. Choose a leadership development resource (perhaps one mentioned in this chapter) and read more about your style. In what areas do you and your fellow team members feel you need to improve?

4. Make time this week to completely review your organizational chart. Schedule a meeting with your team to assess whether you have too many people or too few people. Based on the DNA of Hall of Fame Leadership (Chapter 2) and the Six Benchmarks for Internal and Intentional Leadership (Chapter 3), are all corporate family members fulfilling their obligations to the organization?

*Chapter*S I X

Developing Your
High Performance Team

I don't care if you sell Coca-Cola, Compaq Computers, or Q-Tips. If you're in business, trust is your best product.

Lou Holtz

The process of developing your High Performance Team is both internal and intentional. Internally speaking, *your transformation* is as much a part of the process as is the actual fielding (Chapter 5), developing (our current topic), and maintaining (Chapter 7) of your High Performance Team. In other words, as you grow and develop professionally, so will your organization and your team. The changes that you have made by fielding your HPT are also an intentional effort as you've reorganized current employees and

> The process of developing your High Performance Team is both internal and intentional.

recruited new ones to fill needed roles and responsibilities. And, as always, we recommend that these "straight line" strategies be accomplished with internal and intentional thought and effort.

> High Performance Team members must receive regular leadership development.

It's with these two descriptors in mind—*internal* and *intentional*—that we'd like you to start strategizing about how you can develop the High Performance Team you've gathered. As a leader, your job will be to take these individuals and actively shape their leadership skills. You must also role model these leadership skill sets yourself.

One of the biggest mistakes we see leaders make is assuming that once they've put the time and energy into fielding a group full of hot shots, go-getters, and cutting-edge team members, they are going to stay that way. Unfortunately, they're missing a critical component of the leading edge to success: *High Performance Team members must receive regular leadership development.* Indeed, as a HPT begins to struggle is often when we receive the emergency call from a confused leader who can't quite figure out what went wrong.

> Leaders must recognize two realities: things go from order to disorder everywhere in our universe (and usually much more quickly than we'd like), and, there is no such thing as perpetual motion with High Performance Teams.

Leaders must recognize two realities: *things go from order to disorder everywhere in our universe (and usually much more quickly than we'd like)*, and, *there is no such thing as perpetual motion with High Performance Teams.* Someone must consistently infuse the necessary energy for equipping peers and subordinates so they can develop exceptional leadership skills. Then, and only then, will this team be able to attain the leading edge in all aspects of life.

The "order to disorder" principle comes directly from Newton's 2nd Law of Thermodynamics, which is considered a law of the universe for a reason: there is NO possibility that a system, including your organization, will stay the same. Things get worse when no energy is put into that system. The good news is that the opposite is true when we do put time, energy, and effort into programs, products, and people. *Chaos can be overruled with internal and intentional intervention!*

> There is NO possibility that a system, including your organization, will stay the same.

And guess who we're asking to do that? Yes—you, the Leader! If you don't actively implement these personal and professional strategies, your employees will be less likely to take up the course.

Sometimes companies try a quick fix approach to keep their HPT working together, often by using a "flavor of the month" leadership development technique. These fads usually fall short because nothing can replace sound skill sets that are developed *over time.* You've probably been to enough of the "hug a tree" or "ride the river" team building seminars to know that they can be fun (or maybe not) while you're doing them, but

> Chaos can be overruled with internal and intentional intervention!

overall take-away is minimal. Ten days later, most of what you may have learned has faded to faint memory, and no lasting transformation remains that truly impacts the way you lead others.

So, how do you get started developing the lasting High Performance Team that you've fielded? We have eight specific **Action Plans** that will get you from where you are now to where you'd like your team and organization to be. These Action Plans are inter-connected, like links on a chain. If one is weak, the chain won't be strong. If all links are healthy, then the connections should hold under all kinds of pressure. In order to create these powerful bonds within your HPT, you must be willing to implement the following plans:

+ *Action Plan #1*: Develop the rapport of your HPT members
+ *Action Plan #2*: Build a high level of trust
+ *Action Plan #3*: Assist and insist that all team members interact and communicate at a high Level
+ *Action Plan #4*: Demand that your HPT learn to resolve conflict
+ *Action Plan #5*: Set the standards for mutual accountability between corporate family members.
+ *Action Plan #6*: Practice the techniques needed for team unity
+ *Action Plan #7*: Encourage HPT members to problem solve and execute initiatives
+ *Action Plan #8*: Resolve stress at all levels of your corporate family

We'd like to expand on each of these Action Plans, but before we do, we want to offer a word of caution. While some members of your High Performance Team may be resistant to your efforts to develop their skill sets, whether in the area of technical or leadership abilities, it is still your job to move them beyond their current comfort zone. You may get such negative feedback as, "Hey, you hired me because I'm the best; why are you trying to change a good thing?" And members of your team that have been at the company for some time may not like the idea of change in any area, especially when it affects them. *Resistance becomes one of the most difficult challenges as leaders attempt to develop their HPT.*

> Resistance becomes one of the most difficult challenges as leaders attempt to develop their HPT.

There's a saying about the biggest room in the world—it's the room for improvement. All of us need improvement, including your hot shots. If you can pass this lesson on to all employees now, letting them know that you're also equally open to new ideas and change, the process of developing your teams and organization will be all the easier as you continue down the path toward peak performance.

ACTION PLAN #1: DEVELOP THE RAPPORT OF YOUR HPT MEMBERS

The Setting: A wedding reception
The Participants: Family and friends from all walks of life
The Dilemma: To bring everyone together so they can enjoy the celebration

We've all been to one—the infamous wedding reception. It's a time to celebrate, but it's also uncomfortable. There will be family members present, and some of them may not get along well or ever spend much time together. The friends joining the party come from all sorts of backgrounds, experiences, and walks of life. How do you encourage this diverse company of people to be comfortable enough to celebrate during a wonderful occasion?

Well, traditionally this is done with the assistance of lots of food, drinks, and dancing! Getting this multifaceted mix of guests to dance together is the centerpiece to a great experience for everyone. And as a leader, the same is true for you. You must get the members of your High Performance Team to "dance." You should orchestrate the experiences that help the members of your corporate family to build rapport with one another.

> You must get the members of your High Performance Team to dance.

When LEADon begins to work with organizations, our first activities always include rapport builders. The word rapport comes from the French, *raport* which literally means "to bring back." In modern terms we would define this as agreement, accord, or harmony. Rapport building is about developing the relationships of team members. It gives them chances to talk about topics they might never have the opportunity to discuss during the course of a regular business day. Rapport building also provides men and women time to interact and to get to know one another as people—not just professionals—so they start to develop a level of connectedness that you, their leader, can build on in the days ahead. Over time, trust develops, and trust will bring down barriers.

You must also understand a basic principle: people are relationship-oriented. At LEADon, we firmly believe that relationships are the center of the universe—and without relationship nothing else we do really

> Relationships are the center of the universe—and without relationship nothing else we do really matters.

matters. Think about that for a minute. If you are working with people, and people are wired for relationships, then part of your leadership time and energy must be focused on building and developing those relational skills.

You will need to provide opportunities for your team members to get to know one another in informal activities and meetings. You can coordinate the rapport building, or you may want to bring in experienced facilitators so you can be part of the process too. As most leadership experts would agree, the main objective during this time should be "to have participants become acquainted and mix together. This helps support the early stages of the group's development as members build a sense of comfort, as well as a sense of belonging" (Ukens, 2000, p. 2).

> Relational Equity may be the most valuable commodity that any organization obtains.

Whether you plan a dinner party or a meet and greet session, actively strategize ways that you can get your HPT members together so that "Relational Equity" can begin to be built. Relational Equity may be the most valuable commodity that any organization obtains. While you may not be able to list it as a business asset or add it to your balance sheet, it's invaluable and truly impacts every other item that you find there!

ACTION PLAN #2:
BUILD A HIGH LEVEL OF TRUST

Sam Collins, a C-level executive for a small, successful firm, contacted us after a downward trend in his company continued into a third quarter. Sam had sensed that a growing level of distrust among employees was contributing to more and more losses for his organization. After an initial meeting with Sam, we discovered the main cause of the distrust. The new CEO, a replacement hired by corporate headquarters for the one who had just retired, had created an environment of competition among staff rather than cooperation. Several employees, including members of the leadership team, repeated the CEOs new mantra: "Watch out because I can replace any of you with someone else!"

No wonder this company was beginning to show signs of failure. The CEO didn't understand that trust is the next link in the Relational Equity chain that leads to solid development of High Performance Teams. Once a group gains rapport, that relationship must move to a deeper level in order to grow and be sustained over time. "The essence of a cohesive leadership team is trust, which is marked by an absence of politics, unnecessary anxiety, and wasted energy" (Lencioni, 2000, p. 143). Basically it's like saying, "I am not afraid of you, and you don't have to be afraid of me. I can tell you important information, and vice versa. We commit to mutual improvement, and neither of us will violate that trust by taking information to others who might misuse it."

There are three specific descriptors that we use for trust: *open, vulnerable, and transparent.* When someone is open, they are approachable and regularly available. Vulnerability is a humble honesty that isn't afraid to admit weaknesses, fear, mistakes, or failures. Transparency involves sharing the "real" you (who you truly are) versus the "ideal" you (who you want others to think you are). "Your leadership strengths—what you want to preserve—lie at the intersection of where your real self matches your ideal" (Goleman, Boyatzis, & McKee, 2002, p. 134).

As the leader of your HPT, you set the tone for trust in your organization. If you're approachable and open, men and women in your corporate family will learn that this is a value to be upheld. When you are vulnerable, co-workers will be able to relate to you because, after all, they have their own weaknesses, fears, and failures. And when you're transparent and allow team members and subordinates to see the real you, then they'll feel more and more comfortable with being real as well. As you provide opportunities for your HPT to be honest, share ideas freely, and even admit mistakes, trust will develop over time.

The better you and your HPT become at being vulnerable with one another, higher and higher levels of performance will be attained. Complete levels of trust in organizations are rare and difficult to achieve, in part because adults have an innate self-preservation mode that competes with the desire to be more relational (notice that this is as true in our personal lives as it is in our professional ones). "The boss, leader, parent, or friend who can be vulnerable enough to show that he or she has felt similar things and has made it through or overcome in some way is the one who gains our trust" (Cloud, 2006, p. 94)

As a leader, you have the opportunity to rise above the basic way people tend to do business and make yourself and your organization better than ever. The style that Sam's boss chose led to the dysfunction of the team. *Developing trust over time will not only reduce dysfunction but also develop employees into true corporate family members who work cooperatively for everyone's ultimate success.*

Lou Holtz, considered by many to be one of the best college football coaches of all time, knows a few things about developing HPTs. His quote at the beginning of the chapter sums our thoughts up perfectly: No matter what your business may be, trust is your best product!

ACTION PLAN #3: ASSIST AND INSIST THAT ALL TEAM MEMBERS INTERACT AND COMMUNICATE AT A HIGH LEVEL

Part I discussed Personal Strategies for communication in leadership, that is, those skills that *you* need to become an exceptional leader. Now that we are working on your Professional Strategies in Part II, we're asking you to take those skill sets and pass them on to your HPT members. And, to be quite honest, we really cannot emphasize the ability to communicate enough. It is a major theme of the LEADon philosophy—a straight line to improving performance that must be revisited and re-emphasized over and over again.

Communication is vital based on what we discussed in Action Plan #2: people are relational; relationships are developed through interacting and communicating with one another. To fully develop your HPT, all members must get comfortable relating on a real-time basis about all of the things that matter most. We're not talking about superficial small talk, but honest, deep, heart-to-heart interactions.

> The benefit of the scuba-perspective in relationship-building is that the world under the surface is far more rich and diverse than the one at the surface.

If we described this in terms of a sporting activity, we'd say that instead of being snorkelers, your corporate family members should all become expert scuba-divers. As you know, snorkeling involves staying at the surface—skimming by and sticking to where we land-lovers are more comfortable. Scuba-diving involves taking risks and going deeper than we probably feel comfortable. The benefit of the scuba-perspective in relationship-building is that the world under the surface is far more rich and diverse than the one at the surface. Because of this, the potential for new ideas, new insights, and new opportunities is virtually unlimited.

Here are a few ways your HPT can communicate at a deep level:

with Clarity
with Connectedness
with Purpose
with Goals
with Honesty
with Challenges
with Passion

Perhaps the most difficult of these is clarity. Clarity infers the absence of assumptions and ambiguity. If this is true, then it could be frightening to think about how often you are truly clear. How often does your communication with others (including those in your personal life) leave no room for assumptions? If we're all completely honest, we have to admit that clarity is a struggle at least sometimes. It's like the old game of telephone—you give a sentence to someone at the beginning of a line, then each person tries to repeat it until the message reaches the last person. By the end of the line, the original sentence is completely boggled. We did this during one leadership training with over one hundred men and women. The original sentence was "Nuclear bombs caused tremendous devastation in WWII," but when the last person shared what she had heard, it morphed to, "Brad Pitt has cute buns." Unbelievable, right? Well, it begins to make more sense when you consider the human potential to hear what we want to hear, miss parts we don't really pay attention to, and sometimes even change information to suit our own fancy.

So, the clearer you are, the better for everyone involved. As you practice clarity in communication with your HPT members, they'll have a better understanding of what it means to give each other exactly what they need to know every time. Connectedness will bring the past, present, and future of the team together, while purpose will allow the team to have a specific, common direction. By defining goals, targets are set that the entire team understands. Honesty speaks to the integrity of the team—and it increases the credibility of all communicators. Any High Performance Team that sets clear-cut expectations will ensure that all members stretch and accomplish the goals and mission. Also, when members of the corporate family speak with passion, this fuels the entire team toward success.

> As you practice clarity in communication with your HPT members, they'll have a better understanding of what it means to give each other exactly what they need to know every time.

Think about how you'd like to see your HPT interacting and communicating. You have a choice to allow them to work in the same way you have experienced workplace relationships in previous organizations or to do things differently—hopefully even better than you've ever seen things done before. Attaining the leading edge with the key ingredient of communication must be an intentional developmental process. Regrettably, many of us have acquired ineffective skill sets along life's journey. In one survey of 1000 U.S. workers, 42% reported incidences of yelling and other kinds of verbal abuse at work (Marino, 2000). While we may say this is unacceptable, how many of us can relate to that 42% group?

Your leadership in communicating is also critical because we live in a world where the methods of communication are rapidly evolving. From Internet blogging to texting to "twit-tering," people are connected in more ways than ever before. In particular, the younger members of your corporate family—Gen Xers and Millenials—are in a virtually constant state of connect-edness! While we'll discuss more about how to lead these two generational groups later (see Chapter 9), suffice it to say that leaders must strive to interact and communicate with these corporate family members—sometimes in ways that are new to them—if they want to keep them engaged and eager to stay part of the organization.

> Keep the lines of communication open, and help your HPT learn ways to connect and interact— internally and intentionally.

The bottom line for exceptional leadership: *Keep the lines of communication open, and help your HPT learn ways to connect and interact—internally and intentionally.*

ACTION PLAN #4: DEMAND THAT YOUR HPT LEARN TO RESOLVE CONFLICT

Every organization deals with conflict. We believe that the more successful you are, the more conflict you will encounter. This is simply par for the course when you have people working together because they will have conflicting views, conflicting ways of doing things, and conflicting methods of dealing with conflict itself. We like what Lencioni points out: "cohesive teams fight. But they fight about issues, not personalities. Most important, when they are done

> We believe that the more successful you are, the more conflict you will encounter.

fighting, they have an amazing capacity to move on to the next issue, with no residual feelings" (2000, p. 145). We believe that any HPT that aspires to attain the leading edge should and does adopt a set of values about how conflict will be resolved. All team members must be willing to subordinate to this value system in every single circumstance.

> We believe that any HPT that aspires to attain the leading edge should and does adopt a set of values about how conflict will be resolved.

Tina Alvarez was a member of a leadership team that didn't have any system for conflict resolution in place, in part because the chief executive preferred to create conflict rather than resolve it. You see, Vince was a yeller and rather than use the intercom system, he shouted orders out his door to the leadership team, his office manager, and the receptionist down the hall. He hollered out directives, and he screamed insults when he was angry.

Several members of the leadership team actually took prescription medication to handle the constant conflict and stress that Vince stirred up. He often pitted his employees against each other when business goals had not been attained. One lawsuit was looming from an employee who had left the organization under duress, and another had just been resolved. Both legal battles only added fuel to Vince's fire and his desire to let off steam through abusing others. Tina was secretly looking for a position elsewhere since her co-workers had refused her suggestion to confront Vince and make a stand for the good of the company and its 250 employees.

The links in the "Relational Equity" chain of this organization were broken long ago, and no one seemed to have any energy left to stop the corporate bleeding. This is what constant conflict does, hopefully not to such an extreme, but its subtle powers are destructive nonetheless. Consider your organization for a few minutes. As a leader, how do you resolve conflict when it arises? Does your company have a system in place that helps you and members of your HPT deal with problems and differences? If not, you may find that the high performance of the team will not last very long.

The rapport and trust you're developing will form a firm foundation for your corporate family members so they can feel comfortable with resolving conflict in appropriate ways. In addition, keeping the lines of communication open (which starts with you, by the way) and encouraging team members to interact on a regular, real time basis are also important.

> The rapport and trust you're developing will form a firm foundation for your corporate family members so they can feel comfortable with resolving conflict in appropriate ways.

LEADon teaches twelve specific steps to conflict resolution to leaders and their teams. It is critical that everyone agrees to a value system for resolving conflict and strategically utilizes it when conflicts do occur. "In those instances when a fight gets out of hand and drifts over the line into personal territory—and this inevitably happens—the entire team works to make things right" (Lencioni, 2000, p. 145). As the leader, how you handle conflict will be the primary example others will follow, and as you teach appropriate conflict resolution skills to your corporate family members, you will encourage a positive, productive working environment.

ACTION PLAN #5: SET THE STANDARDS FOR MUTUAL ACCOUNTABILITY BETWEEN CORPORATE FAMILY MEMBERS

Recently, discussions about policy and procedures in regard to accountability have been at an all-time high. Ironically, problems with accountability have also risen dramatically. Dishonesty and corruption in business, politics, and society in general during the past several decades have shaken up everyone from Main Street to Wall Street.

Even those who sincerely want accountability often struggle with making this process a reality. Though counter-productive, one reason it's so difficult is that many men and women have a natural desire to be liked, so they don't want to upset others by confronting them with issues that need to be addressed. This fear of rejection leads into the next struggle that people have with accountability: the propensity to avoid conflict at all costs. Some individuals are "fight-oriented;" confrontation is no problem for them. They actually need some form of conflict to feel right about their day, but others are "flight-oriented;" they'd rather flee the scene of a conflict than stay and battle it out. The desire to be liked and both the overuse and the avoidance of conflict can negatively impact the establishment of mutual accountability and trust.

> Accountability means being responsible to somebody or something. In your organization, teams must commit to standards of performance and hold one another to them.

Accountability means being responsible to somebody or something. In your organization, teams must commit to standards of performance and hold one another to them. Fortunately, this does not mean that the leader is the lone enforcer of those standards. In fact, High Performance Teams work best when there is *mutual responsibility* between the corporate family members. In addition to the standards, your employees should also hold one another accountable for the execution and results of your business plan.

Mutual, or lateral, accountability is so successful because it's far more difficult for people to hide from their many fellow team members than from the one. "In hierarchical systems, it is easy to get away with superficial compliance or even subtle sabotage. In the interactive system…it is impossible to get away with not being noticed" (Fullan, 2001, p. 118). Fullan goes on to explain that accountability is aided by a healthy dose of peer pressure, as well as a tremendous amount of peer support and collaboration in organizations that insist upon established mutual accountability. *Accountability enhances a cooperative, instead of competitive, work environment for your HPT.*

> Accountability enhances a cooperative, instead of competitive, work environment for your HPT.

One of the worst situations LEADon has encountered involved a family-owned and operated business where employees thought that the meaning of accountability had something to do with taxes and the IRS. No kidding! So, everyone on the payroll felt that fulfilling his or her respective job was plenty of accountability. And when the president of the company took money from the company safe to spend on a trip in the Bahamas, nobody blinked. When a member of the leadership team needed a new car, a check was issued from the business account. None of the executives saw a problem with this personal expense coming from the company funds. Materials and supplies were also constantly disappearing from the warehouse. Evidently the leaders' lack of accountability had been passed on to the rest of the corporate family.

We've seen many leaders readily adopt new measures of accountability and witness the marked improvement in the overall success of their organizations. Several executives we've worked with have held specific company-wide meetings to brainstorm standards for accountability that everyone was willing to live by. In addition, they got buy-in for upholding those standards, helping all employees realize that accountability is a value that should never be violated.

ACTION PLAN #6: PRACTICE THE TECHNIQUES NEEDED FOR TEAM UNITY

Have you noticed the links of the "Relational Equity" chain for developing your High Performance Team forming a unifying, straight line strategy? We started with *rapport* which naturally leads to *trust*. Next to these we laid down *good interaction* and *communication*, which ultimately help with *conflict resolution*. Once *mutual accountability* is in place, your team can't help but become *more unified!*

> Unity doesn't mean union, unanimity, or uniformity.

And that's exactly what exceptional leaders should expect from any High Performance Team.

Unity is all about being there for one another (and, once again, this should be equally true in our personal as well as professional interactions). "You must work together not only to cover each other's backs, but also to cohesively pursue and defeat the opposing forces in your lives" (Jenson, 2006, p. 122). Unity doesn't mean union, unanimity, or uniformity. You don't have to lose yourself or your beliefs in order to be unified;

rather, *unity means that individual team members will always subordinate their agendas to what is best for the team.*

As a leader, your straight line strategy for developing a HPT must have a common thread of unity. Without it, your team will never be as successful and significant as it could be. HPTs function at peak performance when they're united in actions and corporate spirit. Indeed, these teams can be measured by their cohesiveness, especially when conflict and disagreements arise. We understand this won't be accomplished easily, particularly when you have a team of hot shots, go-getters, and cut-

> Unity means that individual team members will always subordinate their agendas to what is best for the team.

ting-edge players, but we promise it's attainable as you work to bring all members of your corporate family together.

We know this to be true based on a four billion dollar public company we worked with some time ago. The executive team of twenty high-powered, gifted individuals ran this worldwide business of 6000 employees. But each leader was so enamored with his or her gifts and abilities that it was hard to see those of anyone else on the team. Many acted as if they were the only key members on the team, so the work environment was kind of like a sporting event fielded by All-Stars, each player wanting to run the show, make the shots, score the points…well, you get the picture.

When LEADon finally entered, this "team" was embroiled in conflict. After establishing monthly meetings where all leaders were encouraged to listen to the other stars in the group (some of them realizing for the first time that they, indeed, *had* other members on the team with expertise in areas they could utilize), we helped them establish their own Action Plan for improving group unity.

Thirty percent of the team decided to leave the company within a few months, unable to handle the fact that they were no longer the main attraction. However, these men and women were replaced by leaders who fit the new culture of the company, and the new corporate family members were team players who valued the unity of their High Performance Team!

> "I need you, you need me"

As you're beginning to encourage more unity in your organization, here are a few concepts to consider:

Uplift one another (encourage routinely—daily)

Need one another ("I need you, you need me")

Intimately relate to one another ("Relational Equity" — that "Center of the Universe" experience we've been talking about)

Trust one another (Trust is a must for High Performing Teams!)

Yield to one another (with humility, be willing to put others before yourself) (Jenson, 2006).

One quick note on that final point: To some executives, we know that humility seems counterintuitive to good leadership, but if this has been your perspective, you need to change your paradigm! Humility isn't a weakness; it doesn't mean you have to be meek and mild. In reality, it shows great strength to be able to admit that you might not be 100% perfect, that you need ideas and assistance, and that you've got room to grow.

> Trust is a must for High Performing Teams!

Look for ways that you can *internally* and *intentionally* build the bonds of unity in your HPT today. Everyone needs uplifting, so start by saying something positive to your key colleagues and subordinates this week. Recognize high-performing employees on a regular basis. Let everyone, from the receptionist to your secretary to the custodian, know they're needed and appreciated. Trust your team by being open and vulnerable. And be one of the first to yield to the ideas of others, especially when they benefit the entire corporate family.

ACTION PLAN #7: ENCOURAGE HPT MEMBERS TO PROBLEM SOLVE AND EXECUTE INITIATIVES

Few people are more frustrating than those who simply can't make a decision. We see this in every facet of society, from our family members to friends to corporate figureheads. We observed a mundane, but nonetheless common example of this while we waited to catch a plane early one Monday morning. The airport Starbucks was packed, the line of customers extending out into the corridor bustling with harried passengers. One, lone patron held up the line of twenty-plus people who were quickly growing impatient, because he couldn't decide between tall or grande, decaf or caffeinated, non-fat or regular milk, and whether or not his Mocha needed whipped cream.

If this businessman's struggle with his morning cup of coffee was any indicator of the rest of his decision-making abilities, he was in serious trouble. But as funny as this scenario is, especially to those of us who have been in line behind that man, we all know certain individuals who go through life overwhelmed by basic decisions, and some of these men and women may be part of our not-so-high performing teams.

Now, before we hit these corporate family members too hard, we must do a bit of self-examination. As leaders, we're often part of the problem. Our generation of high-powered humans have become more than "helicopter parents;" this is a term used for those of us who hover over our children throughout their lives, trying to protect them from everything that might cross their paths and cause pain. *We have become "helicopter leaders."* So when someone struggles, helicopter leaders (for instance, those with the Pacesetting style discussed in Chapter 5) tend to jump in and pick up the slack, denying our weaker members growth through experience. This tendency teaches employees (or kids, or a spouse, or friends) that if they have problems, their leader will simply step in and take over the situation. If this is so, there's no reason for them to bother trying to fix the dilemma themselves.

Exceptional leaders who want to develop exceptionally high performing teams must allow them to problem solve and execute decisions on their own. Here are the four basic steps to effective problem solving:

+ Recognize the Real Problem
+ Analyze the Cause
+ Find Solutions to the Problem
+ Develop an Appropriate Plan of Action

As the leader of your HPT, you should teach this 4-step process to team members and provide scenarios to practice together. This will not only give your team opportunities to hone problem-solving abilities, but it will also give you confidence that your staff is capable of resolving issues on their own. Specifically, you can enlighten them with the 80/20 rule. Taken from the Pareto Principle of Economics (Koch, 2001), the 80/20 rule says that about 20% of the problems we encounter are only the "tip of the iceberg" of what is truly occurring. The remaining 80% is always below the surface, with hidden dangers and dilemmas that must be uncovered first before any action plan can be implemented. This knowledge is vital to employees understanding each other and being able to curb conflict by recognizing the signs of unrest early on.

The problem-solving process is also where you can strengthen the unity that you've been developing in your HPT. It's critical that members of the team understand that other players also have insights to the everyday problems. By recruiting others to analyze the cause(s) and find solutions, a winning plan of action will be easier to develop. Two minds are better than one, and three, five, or twelve only increase the chances of success.

> About 20% of the problems we encounter are only the "tip of the iceberg" of what is truly occurring. The remaining 80% is always below the surface, with hidden dangers and dilemmas that must be uncovered first before any action plan can be implemented.

Of course, even the most carefully laid plans are useless unless executed. More strategies fail as a result of poor execution, not poor strategic planning. Think about when this may have happened in your organization, or with previous jobs. There could have been great planning sessions in which were found terrific solutions, and even the placement of an amazing action plan, but the problem was never resolved because the plan was never executed. We see this failure to execute plans in problem-solving in many aspects of business.

> More strategies fail as a result of poor execution, not poor strategic planning.

One non-profit organization we worked with realized that they needed to improve their marketing. After a committee was formed, the group reported on the best method for the least amount of money to solve their need for increased public awareness. Months went by as the committee gathered more information, contacted other businesses, and developed a specific marketing strategy. The result was that nothing ever happened, because the group was never empowered by the CEO to execute the plan. Instead, months of research was filed in a large folder and placed on a shelf somewhere at corporate headquarters.

Leaders, we MUST give our people the power to execute plans or we are wasting time, talent, energy, and resources! Even worse, we are setting a precedence for failed execution of future endeavors. Encouraging your HPT members to problem solve and executive initiatives adds a powerful link to the Relational Equity chain you are developing.

> Leaders, we MUST give our people the power to execute plans or we are wasting time, talent, energy, and resources!

Of course, it's the job of leaders to provide accountability standards for problem solving and execution, but this, too, can be accomplished laterally. HPTs should be able to work together for the good of the entire organization. "Giving employees the power to make decisions on their own is the opposite of being rule-bound and hierarchical. And much like believing in people, it has the effect of making people behave more considerately and generously" (Haughton, 2004, p. 152).

ACTION PLAN #8: RESOLVE STRESS AT ALL LEVELS OF YOUR CORPORATE FAMILY

At this point in *The Leading Edge,* you may be wondering why you should worry about other people's stress since you have so much on your own plate—including worrying about how to develop those high performers into the winning team you want and need.

Eleanor Roosevelt had firsthand experience with the difficulties and stresses related to leadership, and she knew all-too-well the potential consequences of overwhelming pressures. When Harry Truman offered her assistance after the death of her husband, she gave him a surprising answer: "Is there anything we can do for you? For you are the one in trouble now" (Torricelli, 2001, p. 158). For you, as a leader in your organization, stress is inevitable; it goes hand-in-hand with your role and responsibilities. How you deal with tension and pressures will powerfully impact you, your corporate family members, and your organization.

> **75% of all time lost in the workplace is stress-related.**

You may be amazed to learn that *75% of all time lost in the workplace is stress-related.* (Covey, October 1999). Stress impacts how members of our corporate family function at work, and how they represent the company when they aren't at work. Unhappy employees can't and don't hide it; everyone in their world knows about it. And we wonder sometimes why we have a hard time recruiting new people to our organizations!

Job stress also hurts our bottom line. According to one report, pressures at work costs the U.S. economy up to *$300 billion annually* (The American Institute of Stress, June, 2009). This is due in part to accidents, absenteeism, employee turnover, diminished productivity, medical and legal problems, and workman's compensation. Sadly, the number of stressed-out employees continues to climb in every industry across this nation.

First, it's important that leaders understand that pressure is a normal part of life—without it we wouldn't function as well as we should, particularly when an emergency occurs or a matter needs immediate attention. But compounded stress, day after day after day, only serves to cause havoc emotionally, physically, and mentally. Our bodies are designed to handle certain amounts of tension, but beyond normal limits, they start to break down.

Second, just because you're a leader doesn't mean you have to handle more stress than anyone else on your team. On the contrary, you must serve as the role-model of how to effectively deal with problems and pressure. Rather than distress, we recommend "eustress." Eustress is the perfect balance point between distress from under- or over-stimulation. Boredom, fatigue, frustration, and dissatisfaction are under-stimulating circumstances. Over-stimulation includes ineffective problem solving, exhaustion, illness, and low self-esteem. The perfect balance point, however, is represented by these key markers:

> Eustress is the perfect balance point between distress from under- or over-stimulation.

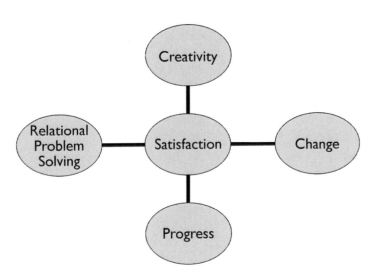

Consider yourself for a moment. How creative do you feel most days? Are you able to solve problems relationally—that is, with the help and input of others? Do you view your career and home life progressing as you'd like it to? Change can feel good or bad, depending on the circumstances, but balanced leaders should see more positive changes over time than negative ones. And, of course, your sense of satisfaction will be representative of how you feel about everything else in life. You and the members of your HPT must strive to keep balance when it comes to stress; you need to intentionally seek to "eustress" rather than to stress. Interestingly, stress itself is not the problem. Rather, stress gives you a choice to either become distressed (poor, destructive responses) or to eustress (productive responses). The following are a few ways to find balance despite daily stresses:

+ Exercise regularly.
+ Get as much sleep as *your* body needs.
+ Make time for family and friends.
+ Learn to say no.
+ Become more organized; make a to-do-list, and do those things one by one.
+ Try to be more positive.
+ Take time to play each week.
+ Laugh more.

Some of these techniques may seem simple, but try applying them for a week and see how you do. Many executives and leaders *know* what they should do, but most fail to follow through because they are too busy and too stressed! If you can't implement some of these tactics that will improve your level of stress, you likely won't be able to help your HPT develop these skills.

You've certainly got plenty to think about at this juncture of our journey. How are you doing with the Action Plans for Relational Equity? If you've struggled with some of the links of the chain, don't get bogged down. Take time to glance at your weakness, but then gaze at your strengths. The journey is a road to be traveled one step at a time. Let's continue the trip together in the next chapter by discovering how to maintain your high performing team.

> Take time to glance at your weakness, but then gaze at your strengths.

SHARPENING YOUR EDGE

1. Review the list of the eight Action Plans. Identify the Action Plans that are crucial for the success of your HPT. Revise this list with the members of your team, and determine what strategies are necessary to improve the performance of your organization.

2. Evaluate the rapport in and between members of your corporate family. Do they "dance" well together? Is there a need for intentional effort to build rapport in your team? How will you accomplish this?

3. Open the lines of communication between corporate family members today. You can do this by asking for input from all team members. Create opportunities for face-time at regular intervals. Send e-mails, surveys, and/or newsletters that focus on performance; celebrate victories, milestones, and lessons learned.

4. What set of values are in place for your team's successful resolution of conflict? Is everyone held equally accountable to follow these standards? Are these standards placed in public view? How far are you and your team from successfully resolving conflict as a professional routine? What steps will you take today to improve this routine?

Chapter SEVEN

Maintaining Your High Performance Team

The idea that excellence at performing a complex task requires a critical minimum level of practice surfaces again and again in studies of expertise...researchers have settled on what they believe is the magic number for true expertise: ten thousand hours.

Malcolm Gladwell

Nobody likes to diet. The word alone can send some of us into a downward spiral. We know that hard work, sacrifice, and commitment are going to be involved as well as lots and lots of time. It would be great if the weight we've accumulated would simply melt off in a week, but it won't. That's just part of why diets are so difficult.

But we yearn for that end result—we feel much better. We *look* much better. All of our clothes fit right again, and we even seem to move with ease. Perhaps most of all, we get lots of unexpected attention as people compliment us on our appearance.

If only this flattery would help keep the weight off. If most of us aren't careful, those pounds will creep back on, and then we've got to start the dieting cycle all over again. That is, *unless* we've adopted a great maintenance plan. Dieting is only half the battle when it comes to staying at our ideal weight. Maintenance is the other half. If we put a plan in place to eat correctly and exercise properly, then we can usually maintain that perfect weight for a long time.

This principle is true in many other areas of life. Think about your car. Sure, you may have bought it new, but it won't stay in great shape unless you take care of it. All vehicles need routine maintenance in order to keep running well for years to come. Or how about your home? What would happen if you just let the plumbing problem go for a while, or decided not to fix that leaking roof? Relationships are even more complicated to maintain than cars or houses. If you don't spend time investing in the people in your life, those relationships can't help but become strained or damaged, sometimes beyond repair.

Maintaining your High Performance Team (HPT) is no different than keeping your car running, your house orderly, and your relationships in great shape. Like most areas in life, you simply need a strategic plan in place to ensure this is accomplished. You must understand how your HPT works and then *internally* and *intentionally* engage and sustain the individuals in your care.

> Re-engage and actively implement the Maintenance Plan you and your team desperately need.

Just because you fielded a great team and have been developing their skills (Chapters 5 and 6) doesn't guarantee everyone will continue to perfectly apply new concepts, especially as time passes. The maintenance process must be regular and consistent because you're working with human beings who can fluctuate, flounder, and even fail without routine guidance and encouragement.

THE MAINTENANCE PLAN

As we said above, maintenance is half of the battle that you're waging in your professional life (and in your personal life as well). Even though you may be somewhat weary from this journey of attaining the leading edge, you cannot abdicate your role and responsibilities as leader now. Feel free to take a deep breath, process what you've been learning, and take some time to rest and reflect (refer to Life Balance from Chapter 4), but then re-engage and actively implement the Maintenance Plan you and your team desperately need.

It's important to realize that it's easier to keep the team you've fielded and developed going and growing with a great Maintenance Plan than it is to try to regroup once they've started to unravel. While the maintenance of a diet, a car, or a house is essential, you must also realize that people are even more complex. Men and women tend to do better when they experience regular care, connection, and consistency. Aside from that, in order for your HPT to grow with a constantly changing economy, they must receive regular guidance from you, their leader. This is certainly true when you consider the concept of mastery discussed in the quote above.

> It's important to realize that it's easier to keep the team you've fielded and developed going and growing with a great Maintenance Plan than it is to try to regroup once they've started to unravel.

In his book *Outliers: The Story of Success*, Gladwell points out that mastery only occurs after a large amount of experience and practice. No matter what field researchers investigated, ten thousand hours came up over and over again as the marker for achieving expertise. This averages out to about ten years. "And why ten years? Well, it's roughly how long it takes to put in ten thousand hours of hard practice. Ten thousand hours is the magic number of greatness" (2008, p. 41).

No matter how many hot shots may be on your HPT, they still need a lot of practice to improve in their field and reach their optimum potential. Even though many of them may believe that they're ready to lead now, you know from your own experience that this, too, requires time, energy, and effort. The straight line strategy for you involves actively formulating a Maintenance Plan that will keep your High Performance Team together, working and practicing their skills, and attaining their leading edge potential.

Part of the practice for your team—or, as Gladwell would say, gaining their 10,000 hours—involves the practical aspects of your daily operations. The other part must include equipping them with the leadership skills we've been discussing in *The Leading Edge.* As we've pointed out, this process must be internal as well as intentional, because "practice isn't the thing you do once you're good. It's the thing you do that makes you good" (Gladwell, 2008, p. 42).

Most organizations we work with fall into one of two categories. The first of these can be a dangerous group to be part of:

Group #1: Good Enough: These types of companies feel that they are doing fine with the team that they've fielded. Productivity is pretty good, and so are the profits. Everyone seems to be comfortable with respective roles, although responsibilities are sometimes a problem. Basically, these organizations are on cruise control, and they don't sense that this should change. The problem is that these are often the businesses that don't handle crises very well because their High Performance Teams aren't that high performing, and they haven't equipped corporate family members with the straight line strategies necessary for successful leadership in less than ideal circumstances.

Group #2: Great, But Let's Keep Growing: These organizations also feel good about what they are accomplishing, but they hold to a firm belief that they can always be doing better. Even when productivity and profitability are up, their leaders look for ways to improve the team, the culture, and the overall goals for the corporate family. Leadership development is always part of the equation for these types of companies, and when difficulties arise, leaders directly address problems utilizing sound principles and skill sets they've acquired over time.

The first group is exactly what Collins meant when he wrote, "Good is the enemy of great. And that is one of the key reasons why we have so little that becomes great" (2001, p. 1). Your teams and organization may be good, but they probably won't stay that way, especially without any energy being put into their continued growth. Unless you internally and intentionally work on maintenance, we can guarantee that no one (including you) will ever be able to attain the edge that leads to greatness. *Exceptional leadership does not accept the status quo; great leaders realize they and their teams still have a long way to go!*

> Exceptional leadership does not accept the status quo; great leaders realize they and their teams still have a long way to go!

So, how do you get started with this next straight line strategy for improving your High Performance Team? Let's look at our **Five-Step Maintenance Plan**:

> *Step #1:* Create a Culture of Appreciation
>
> *Step #2:* Equip HPT Members with the Skills to Read and Relate to Others
>
> *Step #3:* Pass on the Process of Transformational Leadership
>
> *Step #4:* Cascade Coaching and Mentoring Skills
>
> *Step #5:* Develop Leaders Instead of Managers

STEP #1: CREATE A CULTURE OF APPRECIATION

For several years, LEADon worked with a large development company that had originally been started by three friends but had blossomed into a bustling organization with offices in ten cities across the United States. The corporate headquarters were located on the West Coast, but as the distance between the other branches grew, so did the discontent among employees. Leaders and subordinates were resigning in increasing numbers at many locations. It's incredible to think that there could possibly be a problem when all ten offices were functioning not only in the black but also with higher than projected profits. The cause?

A lack of appreciation.

Despite all of the hard work, exceptional results, and banner profits, leaders and subordinates alike felt disenfranchised from everyone at the corporate office. They rarely heard a positive word or gratitude, either verbally or in writing, from the three "founding fathers" (who were still quite active in the day-to-day operations at that point), or from the other members on the corporate leadership team. When the branch offices were contacted by the main office, it usually was to point out some problem or error in reporting or even to demand that they beat their already outstanding performance record.

Now, if you are thinking, "What a bunch of babies. Why couldn't they just be happy with doing well? Why are they so needy?" then this section is definitely for you.

> **25% of good employees quit because of a lack of recognition.**

The Gallop Organization discovered that 69% of employees surveyed reported that non-monetary means of acknowledgment provide the best form of motivation for them. The same poll found that 25% of good employees quit because of a lack of recognition (Glanz, 2002). The opposite scenario is also telling: those employees who felt appreciated became more loyal, engaged, and high-performing workers, as was measured by increased sales, improved productivity, enhanced employee retention, and bottom-line profitability. Now that's good rationale for investing some time in appreciating your employees!

Appreciation and recognition should be a regular and consistent practice in your company. Regularly means routinely—preferably on a daily basis. Consistent means that it's done in a similar fashion, not half-hearted for some team members and overwhelmingly positive for others.

Another study reported that 65% of workers say they didn't receive a single word of praise or recognition during the previous year (Nielson, 2005). If this statistic was applied to your organization, that would mean about 2/3 of your staff feels under-appreciated.

In addition to sensing they aren't appreciated, many employees routinely deal with more negative input. The National Education Association reported that it takes at least four positive statements to outweigh every negative comment (www.nea.org). Reflect on your own professional experiences. How often do you hear positive feedback, supportive comments, or words of praise? If you're like most of us, you probably recall the negative critiques more, so remember that each time you're about to throw out a careless criticism to someone on your team.

> Learning to develop a culture of complimenting and appreciation is fundamental for successful leadership.

If you are still unsure about how words of praise or recognition makes such a big difference in your organization, look at this e-mail we received from one employee:

> "_____ left a voicemail that contained the most amazing compliments I've ever received…it is a message I will never ever delete and [I will] use it to inspire me when I'm pushing through business or feeling insecure about my work. It definitely inspires me to make every effort to make sure my work deserves that degree of praise."

This savvy business woman was so encouraged by a single voicemail that she told us she'd "never ever" erase the message. It inspired her then, and she wants to be able to replay it so she'll stay motivated no matter what is going on. That's how much a Culture of Appreciation can impact people!

Learning to develop a culture of complimenting and appreciation is fundamental for successful leadership. This is a critical task for you to undertake, and it's vital that you pass this skill set on to others in your HPT. Just as you are developing a great work environment and comfortable culture for your corporate family members, you must add this important piece of your Maintenance Plan to the daily experiences of your colleagues and subordinates.

According to Dr. Gerald Graham of Wichita State University, here are some of the top motivating techniques for employees (Glanz, 2002):

+ Personal Thanks
+ Written Thanks
+ Promotion for Performance
+ Public Praise
+ Morale-Building Meetings

Interestingly enough, Dr. Graham points out that these are the easier and less expensive ways of motivating people (notice no large pay raise, bigger office, or stock options are mentioned). They also tend to be practiced the least by leaders across the board. There probably are many reasons why, but part of the problem may be that many of us never experienced a Culture of Appreciation that was regular and consistent, and people pass on what they know. If things haven't been modeled for them, how can they be acquired?

By the way, the development company founders fell into the category of companies that feels good about current productivity, but always strives to improve and progress. They knew they had a great thing going, but they also realized some dilemmas formed as the organization grew. With guidance from LEADon, they learned how to change their culture and adopt principles of appreciation. Soon leaders were cascading these skills to the entire corporate family, resulting in positive changes in employee attitudes and improved retention rates. Their annual Employee Satisfaction Survey measured and recorded the quantitative and qualitative growth.

In *Achieving Authentic Success: 10 Timeless Life Principles that Will Maximize Your Real Potential*, Jenson explains that "the place to begin developing unity in relationships is to learn to build up other people" (2006, p. 84). So here are a few final pointers for you on creating this new culture that includes complimenting and appreciation.

First, the words you say or write must be *concrete* (i.e., measurable, quantifiable, and/or specific). This means they should be relative to the person and the situation you're praising him or her about. For instance, "John, I'm so grateful for your effort with the Diamond Point project. Your input at our last meeting helped our client understand where we are headed." This is much better than, "John, you did great last week. Thanks."

Dr. Jenson also recommends that leaders "learn to compliment people by acknowledging them for something that illustrates their personal and character growth" (2006, p. 84). In fact, focusing on a particular *character quality* or a *competency* your organization wants to instill is a good way to begin formulating compliments. "Teri, the polite way that you treat everyone on staff is exemplary. You definitely role-model our core value of showing respect to others," is very specific and encourages that one value. Finally, all of the compliments, thanks, and praise that you give must be *consistent* (i.e., regular and ongoing). You can't give more to the executive team than you do to the rest of the staff. You shouldn't simply praise those who are making things profitable for you right now; look for good things to say about the others that may spur them on to greater effort.

One of the best examples of creating a Culture of Appreciation we've seen is with a construction company. This organization has experienced its share of difficulties over the years, in part due to the nature of the market for construction. One of the leaders, Tony, fought hard to get a leadership development program in place because he realized the organization would suffer without it. Tony always has a positive attitude and truly cares about all members of his corporate family. He makes an effort to affirm his colleagues and co-workers, no matter what position they hold in the organization. Because of his emphasis on creating a Culture of Appreciation, his corporate family members value his leadership and greatly appreciate his efforts on their behalf.

> The best way to develop a man or woman is by appreciation and encouragement.

Charles Schwab said that the best way to develop a man or woman is by appreciation and encouragement. If you want to maintain the HPT that you've worked to field and develop, then you must begin to create a Culture of Appreciation in your organization—starting today. The dividends will be there, believe us, both in the contentment of your co-workers and subordinates and in how you feel about your interactions with others around you.

STEP #2: EQUIP HPT MEMBERS WITH THE SKILLS TO READ AND RELATE TO OTHERS

People can learn to read others by analyzing facial expressions, body positioning, and even intonations in speech. Since Tonya Reiman's analysis on Fox News and the hit television series *Lie to Me*, many individuals across America are becoming increasingly aware that men and women say as much through these other methods as they do the actual words they speak.

Since your HPT is composed of people, you can probably imagine how body language must impact the daily interactions of your organization. That's why it is so vital for you to teach your leaders and staff how to be able to read and relate better to one another. *Reading* is focusing our attention and analysis on others around us, particularly whoever is interacting with us at the moment. *Relating* is the interpersonal part of the Emotional Quotient (Chapter 2) and involves empathizing and seeking understanding. This doesn't mean you have to agree with everyone, but you are willing to accept where they are coming from.

> **The ability to read and relate are essential to maintaining your HPT.**

The ability to read and relate are essential to maintaining your HPT. No matter how great a job you did at fielding or developing this team, if you don't teach them the basics about how to become better in these two crucial areas, barriers and breakdowns in synergy are right around the corner.

For example, we once assisted two executives at a firm who were completely at odds with one another. They each thought the other was disrespectful and never accepted opinions other than his own. One e-mailed us a copy of lengthy letter he was ready to send, berating the other man for numerous picky items that had been bothering him for the past two years. After a quick phone call, we helped the executive see that this message would only add fuel to what was already a blazing fire. Instead, we encouraged a face-to-face meeting with a neutral party to act as a buffer for both of them. This interaction helped resolve some of their problems, but they both need more time to improve their skills in reading and relating to each other correctly.

You can learn to read and relate to others, and pass these strategies on to your team members using these four simple skills:

+ Understand others' perspectives.
+ Become a student of non-verbals.
+ Listen more carefully.
+ Empathize with others.

> Understanding others' perspectives must begin with accepting that people aren't going to be like us, and that our way isn't the best or only way.

People reared in different families in different neighborhoods with differing cultural, socio-economic, religious, and educational experiences are not as similar as we sometimes think. The trouble is that those we view as "others" are going through life thinking pretty much the same thing as us, wondering why we aren't acting, speaking, or thinking the same way they are! That thought often leads all of us to the same conclusion: "They're all mixed up! How could they possibly be thinking that way?"

Understanding others' perspectives must begin with accepting that people aren't going to be like us, and that our way isn't the best or only way. Exceptional leaders should strive to learn how people are different, how they acquired the viewpoints they have, and why they make the decisions they do. And we must help our co-workers and subordinates comprehend that different isn't bad; it's just different.

In the richly diverse society of 21st century America, understanding this is more important than ever. Many of us come from various cultural, ethnic, racial, and religious backgrounds, and the diversity increases because many of our companies do business locally, nationally, and globally. As we learn about others around us, we also learn more about ourselves; "We can get a full view of our own cultures and behaviors only by viewing them from the perspectives of other racial and ethnic cultures" (Banks, 2001, p 46).

As the leader of your HPT, you can model how to better understand others when you interact with people within and outside of your organization. For instance, when an individual says something that you don't understand, ask a clarifying question, such as, "I don't quite know what you meant by that point. Could you please explain it another way for me?" or, "You seem to feel strongly about that. Could you give me a little background that might help me see where you are coming from?" These types of interactions can also be practiced with your corporate family; LEADon has facilitated a number of workshops that dealt specifically with honing skills to improve people's perspectives within corporate settings.

> **93% of what a person communicates to you isn't the words he or she is saying.**

Becoming a student of non-verbals doesn't mean you've got to become an expert in body language, but there certainly are skills that you can work on to improve this critical area of communication. *Experts say that only 7% of communication comprises words. The rest of what people are saying to you is made up of 38% tone and 55% body language.* If you do the math, *this means that 93% of what a person communicates to you isn't the words he or she is saying.* Is it any wonder we struggle to communicate in our professional worlds as well as in our personal lives?

In *Blink: The Power of Thinking Without Thinking*, Gladwell explains how we tend to pick up non-verbals and make judgments based on "the impression we form of other people... we [then] come up with a constant stream of predictions and inferences about what that person is thinking and feeling" (2005, p. 194). One difficulty about these judgments is that they aren't always right. For instance, just because a colleague is frowning doesn't mean he or she is unhappy with you. He or she could be having a bad day in general, or ate something at lunch that didn't settle, or merely has something else on his or her mind at the moment.

According to Ekman and Friesen (1978), there are at least three thousand expressions our faces can make using just two muscles. Taking a look at someone's face to judge their thoughts is challenging enough for experts to figure out, yet we often decide whether to like a person or not based on a quick glance at his or her face. Moreover, often these split-second decisions are filtered through our own prejudices and stereotypes (Gladwell, 2005).

> There are at least three thousand expressions our faces can make using just two muscles.

We can improve our non-verbal reading skills with lots of time and effort. We must learn not to judge solely on first impressions. Non-verbal communication is all about the big picture, so as a leader you need to also look at some of the following:

+ The shape of the whole body (sitting stiffly versus slumped over)
+ The positioning of the body relative to other people and things
+ Movement of the limbs, head, and fingers
+ Micro-movement of muscles (such as twitching)
+ Skin color and texture (flushed cheeks or paleness)
+ Voice pitch
+ Speed of voice
+ Sweating

Realize that non-verbal communication can extend beyond body actions to anything that sends a message. For example, the style, tidiness (or lack thereof), and coordination of clothing can speak volumes. Personal adornment, from jewelry to hair styles to tattoos, can tell you about lifestyle or attitudes. Even items that others own or the way they design their workspace communicates about who an individual is or how he or she wants to be perceived.

> Few of the six billion-plus people on this planet are truly skilled listeners.

Watching for these non-verbal cues is essential in reading and relating to others, but so is *listening more carefully* to others in your world. Few of the six billion-plus people on this planet are truly skilled listeners. There's a saying about God giving us two ears and only one mouth for a reason: it's because we're supposed to do twice as much listening as we do talking.

Listening carefully needs to be an intentional process because it doesn't come easily to most of us. When you listen to a person who is speaking, you should give them your full, undivided attention—not finishing up an e-mail or fiddling with your Blackberry while they speak. You also ought to give appropriate verbal or non-verbal responses as you listen, asking clarifying questions so gaps can be filled in. And most of all, don't try to solve a problem or fix everything when someone comes to share. Sometimes men and women merely need to get things out in the open; they can often figure out a solution on their own. If they need help, they'll ask, or you can check to see if there is anything else they would like from you after the conversation is completed.

Finally, *empathizing with others* involves identifying with them. We're not talking about feeling sorry for someone (sympathy), but attempting to understand where he or she is coming from *with compassion*. If you've ever hit your thumb with a hammer, you know exactly how someone feels who has done the same thing. That's empathy; you *feel* the emotion, the pain, the loss, the joy, the satisfaction, etc. While your circumstances don't have to be exactly the same, you can relate to others by connecting with something in your own life that brings up similar memories or emotions.

While some individuals may think this is too "touchy/feely" for them and their organization, we can assure you that in order to maintain a HPT of complex, interpersonal human beings you *must* relate to them on these levels and help them acquire and build upon these communicative skill sets themselves. When your team can effectively read and relate to one another, you'll have laid a foundation for success no matter what lies ahead.

STEP #3: PASS ON THE PROCESS OF TRANSFORMATIONAL LEADERSHIP

Many leaders that we interact with use a "management" approach to their leadership styles. After all, they were taught management courses while in college or business school. However, managing means controlling, rather than conducting, situations. At LEADon, we prefer to focus on *maintenance;* in other words, leaders are responsible for assisting, guiding, encouraging, supporting, and equipping their staff, rather than commanding them.

Perhaps no other area impacts performance more than acquiring the skills necessary to transform—the

> Leaders are responsible for assisting, guiding, encouraging, supporting, and equipping their staff, rather than commanding them.

ability to adjust and adapt to change. Therefore, a large component of the Maintenance Plan for your HPT must involve taking your transformational leadership abilities and equipping your colleagues and subordinates with these vital skills. At LEADon, we explain that this transformational process must involve the *head, heart, and hands: The "head" or mind* always involves current information and new knowledge. *The "heart"* emphasizes the feelings you have about what you believe, while *the "hands"* are how you and your team actively practice your knowledge and beliefs.

> The "head" or mind always involves current information and new knowledge. The "heart" emphasizes the feelings you have about what you believe, while the "hands" are how you and your team actively practice your knowledge and beliefs.

Much of our work—no matter the field or industry—includes information, or content. These technical skill sets involve *the "head"* and require intelligence and mental intuitiveness. Obviously, keeping up on current content is important because unless we are proficient in our areas of expertise, we will not be as competitive as we should be, and we may not last long in a constantly changing marketplace. As an exceptional leader, you must help your High Performance Team learn how to take their content and adapt to become totally competent. "Effective leaders understand the value and role of knowledge creation; they make it a priority and set about establishing and reinforcing habits of knowledge exchange among organizational members" (Fullan, 2001, p. 87). In other words, maintaining team members involves stimulating creativity, providing opportunity for conversations among co-workers, and assisting all corporate family members with "habit formation."

While we'll talk more about habit formation shortly, the key point about these "head" activities is that your HPT becomes cognizant of the most up-to-date information in your industry, and you are the one that must be certain that this is provided for them (through materials, training, improved technology, etc). In addition, they should comprehend the meaning of the content, and they must move from *opinions about* to *commitment to* the new content. This process allows your High Performance Team to be fully aligned.

The "heart" of the transformational process means allowing yourself and others to *feel* what you believe. "The ethic in companies with strong cultures is 'we'll succeed because we're special'" (Deal & Kennedy, 1982, p. 141). This concept of uniqueness is not part of the information, content, or new knowledge of any company; instead, it's a feeling that is formulated and believed by the entire corporate family. As we work with organizations, one of the priorities we have is for leaders to attain an emotional connection to what they do. Then, and only then, will their co-workers and subordinates have any chance of acquiring that same type of commitment.

When corporate family members begin to believe in what they do as well as in one another, they become attuned. As we discussed in Chapter 3, attunement is an attitude of the heart that can say, "Even though I still feel strongly about this matter, I'm going to emotionally commit for the good of the team and the organization." While this doesn't mean you always have to give in or give up your values, it does mean that your attitude has to be one of cooperation.

Finally, you and your team must be willing to put your ideas (content) and beliefs together through practice. This is utilizing *the "hands"* to get the real work done and accomplish the goals and objectives of your business plan. Maintenance skills are most needed in this "hands-on" process. Exceptional leaders "conduct themselves in such a way as to nurture extra effort and initiative from those around them..." (Deal & Kennedy, 1982, p. 141). And one of the best ways to help everyone to experience the transformational process is to aid them learn how to replace bad habits with productive ones.

A habit is something that is acquired through practice; a pattern of behavior that's repeated so often that it becomes typical or "the norm." Productive skills sets that are successfully applied over time not only become replicable, but they also produce a tremendous sense of satisfaction and fulfillment. Thus habit formation is really nothing more than a growth pattern, much like a plant that develops and produces abundantly when cared for properly.

Your HPT should also *regularly* and *consistently* practice your alignment and attunement goals. As we work with all types of leaders, we encourage the *"31 Day Habit Method."* Let us explain: first, you must develop a plan for change. Consider what habit needs to be acquired (better communication skills, working on a Culture of Appreciation, improving conflict resolution), then design a strategy to pursue the change. Next, you allow time to reinforce your plan (maybe a new core value for your company or a unique sales approach). Many experts believe that you need about 21 days to reinforce a new habit (or break an old one), but we've found that a month gives you some extra breathing room—especially because there might be a day or two when you or your co-workers slip back into an old habit or struggle in the middle of implementing the new one. *So, reserve at least four weeks to implement your new plan so everyone can have 31 days to reinforce the new habit.*

Practice is an essential piece of implementing your plan, so don't forget to add in numerous opportunities for you HPT to work on the process of transformation. "If you want to be excellent, you have to develop the habit of being excellent by doing the right things over and over and over…that's why practicing successful habits day in and day out is the most certain way to win over the long term" (Jenson, 2006, p. 19).

Establishing some rewards and consequences is helpful to all human beings. If we know that there is a penalty for error (maybe we have to put money in the company charity jar when profanity slips out), we often try to avoid that at all costs. Likewise, if we sense there's a reward on the way, we're likely to put more effort into our work. *Performance-based compensation incentivizes production.*

Performance-based compensation incentivizes production.

And don't forget the accountability. Get your corporate family members to operate together on this. They can work in pairs or teams, but let them take on this responsibility themselves. When you begin to delegate these types of roles, "employees respond accordingly, accept responsibilities willing, and get on with it" (Deal & Kennedy, 1982, p. 142). Your main role of encouraging (and internalizing correct thinking) will be much easier without feeling the need to be a watchdog of the habit formation process.

Lastly, equipping you and your team is critical. We believe in training and equipping at LEADon—that's what we are all "aligned and attuned to" in our organization. Many companies utilize our services because maintenance is a difficult and complicated process that often requires outside assistance After all, leaders cannot simply give their employees new information and expect them to transform! Why? Because "focusing on information rather than use is why sending individuals and even teams to external training by itself does not work…" (Fullan, 2001, p. 79). The transformational process is a change of the regular course that involves new contexts, new settings, and new ways of sharing what has been learned.

The information you have here is a great place to start. Remember that as an exceptional leader you will be able to maintain your HPT by helping them learn how to transform themselves—internally and intentionally! Pass along the strategies that corporate family members need to include their head, heart and hands so they can be more productive and profitable than ever before.

STEP #4: CASCADE COACHING AND MENTORING SKILLS

Recently we were intrigued by a story we saw on an animal show. An injured buffalo was being stalked by a hungry lion. The wounded animal limped as best as it could, struggling to catch up to the herd, but, before long it became weary and gave up. Everyone watching knew the lion's attack and kill was inevitable. Yet suddenly a shocking turn of events unfolded—the rest of the herd of buffalo turned and began to chase the lion. Startled, it retreated and raced off in the opposite direction. The entire group then returned for their injured comrade, who was re-energized by their efforts and began to run again with them toward safety.

> When members feel supported, they thrive. When individuals know that they are not alone, they're energized.

This is the very essence the effect of good coaching and mentoring has on a team. When members feel supported, they thrive. When individuals know that they are not alone, they're energized. Even if someone is struggling, a group's encouragement may be enough to allow him or her to pick up the pieces, get things together again, and move on successfully toward the future.

So leaders, how do you mentor and coach those around you? Do you energize, mobilize, or motivate? Effective leaders are coaches and mentors to their corporate family members, and they cascade these crucial skill sets down to each and every employee.

When we think about coaching, most of us envision an individual in charge of a sports team. Hang on to that thought because that coach is the type of leader all sorts of teams need in order to survive and thrive. "Coaches help people identify their unique strengths and weaknesses, tying those to their personal and career aspirations" (Goleman, Boyatzis, & McKee, 2002, pp. 60—61). At LEADon, we assist leaders as they strive to help their employees set long-term goals and develop a plan to attain their full potential in the organization.

A good coach will challenge you to identify your priorities, encourage you to establish your long-term vision, and offer the clarity that only an outside influence can give. As a leader, you hopefully had some good coaching along your professional journey, though we know that many have experienced below-average or even non-existent coaching or mentoring. One member of our LEADon team remembers a boss whose idea of coaching was to shout insults, sometimes laced with profanity, to "inspire" employees to work harder and improve their efforts. Of course, all this did was create a negative culture where turnover was high and underlying dissatisfaction even higher.

> Coaching and mentoring go hand-in-hand.

We believe coaching and mentoring go hand-in-hand, even though there are some who define these skill sets differently (MacLennan, 1995). Basically, there are eight tactics that leaders who desire to coach and mentor their HPTs must implement:

✦ Gain clarity.
✦ Set priorities.
✦ Motivate and inspire others to take action.
✦ Teach new skill sets and information.
✦ Challenge people to be their best.
✦ Make everyone accountable.
✦ Provide support at all times.
✦ Remind everyone to celebrate.

Researchers have discovered that most employees only remember about 10% of job instructions when they are *told* what to do. When a leader *told* and *showed*, however, those same workers recalled about 60% of the information. Finally, when those leaders combined telling and showing with *employees actively practicing the skills*, they retained about 90% of the instruction (Hendricks, 1994). This means that your coaching and mentoring relationship must be active, not passive. People learn best by being engaged in the process, and this is true of leaders as well as the rest of the staff.

When Dr. Ron Jenson works with leaders on coaching and mentoring, he recommends the IDEA approach. Basically this method includes:

*I*nstruction

*D*emonstration

*E*xposure to Experience

*A*ssessment

Obviously the "show and tell" described above cover the first two steps, Instruction and Demonstration. The actual practice of the skills you're trying to implement is the Exposure to Experience your co-workers and subordinates need. Your employees should have feedback on how they're doing in order to continue improving in these areas—Assessment.

According to the Center for Management and Organization Effectiveness, "it is increasingly important for managers, directors, supervisors, and senior executives to be good coaches…When a good coach engages his team members in continuous and positive interactions, the developed synergy will produce tremendous results" (Fankhouser, July, 2009).

When you decide to make coaching and mentoring a priority, your HPT will feel the benefits. First, you will continue to improve the overall satisfaction of the individuals on your team as you coach and they learn to assist one another in the process. Second, you will be enhancing the EQ skills we discussed in Chapter 2, and emotionally balanced employees connect better with colleagues and customers alike. The connection from these employees to you, the leader, is another positive bonus: "Most people in business have a special place in their hearts for those…who gave them useful feedback and took enough interest to coach them in their careers" (Haughton, 2004, p. 164).

> Emotionally balanced employees connect better with colleagues and customers alike.

If you're worried about the potential impact that spending time and energy coaching, mentoring, and helping your corporate family members might have on profitability, perhaps what Goleman, Boyatzis, and McKee discovered may put those fears to rest: "the coaching style may not scream 'bottom-line results,' but in a surprisingly indirect way, it delivers them" (2002, p. 63).

STEP #5: DEVELOP LEADERS INSTEAD OF MANAGERS

We hope we don't disappoint you, but you need to know that leaders are not born, they're made. *True* leaders, that is— *exceptional* leaders.

Yes, there are companies (and we've worked with a few) where some members of leadership inherited their positions because they were born into it. For instance, one company is grooming the son to take over for his father in the not-too-distant future. What's exciting for this organization, and all of its employees, is that the young man is quite capable, mainly because the other executives have taken the responsibility upon themselves to coach and mentor him. However, many businesses aren't so diligent. A few years ago, we were hired by a small firm that had a brother-in-law of one of the owners on the executive team. Unfortunately, he probably wouldn't have even been given an entry-level position in any other organization. Not only did he lack the leadership skills necessary to do his current job, but he also had no interest whatsoever in improving. In his mind, the paychecks kept coming, so why bother? His apathy toward development did not make the future very bright for his colleagues.

> Leaders are not born, they're made. True leaders, that is— exceptional leaders.

However, for organizations to attain the leading edge in today's marketplace, leaders need to be developed at all levels, and this process must be maintained throughout their entire career.

Native American culture provides a good example of weighing those who would be leaders appropriately. While a few of their chiefs inherited their roles and responsibilities from their fathers, "in most cases, a chief had to earn his rank in the tribe. He inspired loyalty and respect through wisdom, his record of accomplishments, and the force of his personality" (Freedman, 1987, pp. 8—9). As Gladwell (2008) would summarize, these would-be chiefs had to accumulate their 10,000 hours, too.

We agree with leadership expert Dr. Michael Fullan's opinion about how the best leaders in any time, culture, and institution are developed: "Leaders are not born; they are nurtured" (2001, p. 131). As we mentioned in the section above on trans-

> However, for organizations to attain the leading edge in today's marketplace, leaders need to be developed at all levels, and this process must be maintained throughout their entire career.

formational leadership, your role as leader requires that you also adapt and change despite whatever has happened to you along life's journey; so if you have had a controlling, domineering leader, you must look past your experience and see the present benefits of coaching and mentorship. You have to be equally adaptable as you attempt to "nurture" the members of your HPT and assist them in becoming the leaders of tomorrow.

"Managing" is similar to the controlling leader we've mentioned, and this is not the most productive style for modern-day leaders. Managers tend to control, whereas leaders invite collaboration and completion of initiatives. A leader has a "let's roll" attitude.

> A leader has a "let's roll" attitude.

Notice that "let's" refers to more than the leader taking the reins and running the show. He or she includes the entire group—the whole team at work for the benefit of everyone. A managerial style can't let go of the project, or the business goal, or the client, and allow anyone else on the team to practice. But a good leader (and his or her team) can calmly adapt and transform to meet the changing needs of the economy.

Managers tend to be persistent, hard-working, analytical, intelligent, and tolerant, and they mainly think about today. Leaders, on the other hand, are imaginative, passionate, visionary, risk-taking, consider tomorrow while working today, and are often perceived as brilliant by co-workers. So, given the choice, which do you prefer to be?

Stop a minute to ask how you want your team members to act. Do you want them controlling every situation, or working cooperatively together? Should your team be focused only on the here and now, or would you like them envisioning future plans, hopes, and dreams for your organization? If you prefer the latter, then it's up to you to introduce and model these principles about exceptional leadership, as well as give your High Performance Team opportunities to put them into practice. Remember, though, you are dealing with people, so be patient and kind. As Blanchard points out, "Situational leadership is not something you do to people but something you do with people" (1985, p. 84). Like you, many of your HPT members have experienced a wide array of "leadership" styles—from their homes, communities, educational backgrounds, and business experiences. Some of these may be outstanding, but many will be lacking. Seek to model the outstanding ones so that you, your employees, and your organization can all benefit.

Here are a few ways you might choose to role-model these exceptional leadership skills for your HPT members:

✦ Develop new approaches to longstanding problems and open issues to new options.

✦ Use your vision to excite people and develop choices that make those images real and attainable.

✦ Focus people on shared ideas and raise their expectations.

✦ Work from high-risk platforms rather than mundane positions.

✦ Seek opportunities for change and actively support that change.

If you feel that you still need assistance becoming a better leader so you can impact the members of your HPT, you're not alone. This is one reason there are so many leadership development companies in business today. All of us have blind spots and weaknesses that have developed over time, and sometimes it takes an unbiased, outside source to coach and mentor us out of those to new habits and greater styles of leadership. *But exceptional leaders—those who are attaining the leading edge—don't sit back and wait for others to change or improve, they DO.* Even if the changes they need to make are somewhat daunting, they're up for the challenge. Finally, they accomplish all of this with an intense focus to never give up.

Collins and Porras have discovered that "visionary companies develop, promote, and carefully select managerial talent grown from inside the company to a greater degree than the comparison companies. They do this as a key step in preserving their core" (1994, p. 173). Your HPT members will become stronger as *you* help increase their leadership capabilities, and so will your company. Rather than a group of managers, you'll be grooming leaders who will, in turn, begin cascading these skill sets to others throughout your entire organization.

THE STORY THAT SAYS IT ALL

The tale of Captain Chesley Sullenberger, or "Sully" as he's become known to the world, is the perfect example of attaining a goal by consistent, committed practice. For many of us, if we hadn't seen the television images of his landing an Airbus A320 on the Hudson River we probably wouldn't have believed it. The landing was picture perfect, and everyone—from passengers to crew members—survived.

In an interview after the emergency ditch, Sullenberger shared some very significant insights: "One way of looking at this might be that for 42 years, I've been making small, regular deposits in this bank of experience: education and training. And on January 15th the balance was sufficient so that I could make a very large withdrawal" (Newcott, May–June 2009, p. 52).

Captain Sullenberger got it! His amazing, unprecedented ability was enhanced and enabled by countless hours of practice, practice, and more practice. And when it really counted, when he found himself in the worst situation possible for his field of expertise, it paid off big time!

We're trying to help you catch a glimpse of how Sully viewed and carried out his work now that you're ready to develop a Maintenance Plan for your HPT. You may be tired from the battle on Wall Street or Main Street. Maybe your organization needs more work than you ever imagined when you took on your current leadership position. Perhaps your HPT isn't quite as high-performing as you'd hoped. Or, like Captain Sully, you might be in the worst professional crisis of your life; one that you never dreamed would happen.

Don't give up! Don't surrender! The skill sets that we're guiding you through offer the straight lines you need to become successful in all aspects of life. They also will benefit everyone in your sphere of influence, from home to work to all those in-between. And the hours that you and your HPT are putting in will pay off in dividends well beyond the financial realm. You will find more fulfillment and satisfaction as you put them into practice and as you pass them on to the leaders of tomorrow.

SHARPENING YOUR EDGE

1. Review the Five-Step Maintenance Plan. How do you and your team fit into this plan? Discuss and develop ways you can implement these important steps that will sharpen your edge.

2. Do you and your HPT celebrate your victories? How?

3. Is complimenting part of your daily personal and professional routine? What can you do to make sure that those closest to you regularly and consistently feel appreciated based on the standards discussed in this chapter?

4. What specific efforts do you and your organization employ to ensure that the corporate family is coached and mentored successfully? Determine what pathway coaching and mentoring will occur in your organization.

5. Who are the managers on your team? Who are the leaders on your team? Do they know this? Are you delegating everything possible to others in order to develop their leadership skills?

Part III

3 TEAM STRATEGIES

Chapter E I G H T

Leading the Generations

What ails the youth of today? "*The seed that your Western civilization has sown is sprouting in your youths; they are not especially perverse—they merely show the defects of your whole system of life*"

George Coe

I can't believe how difficult these young people are to deal with," Bud spouted from the back of a room crowded with frustrated associates.

"Those kids don't have much work ethic at all," Hank added.

Judy, who'd been fairly quiet during most of the morning session, finally spoke up, too. "I just don't get where the new employees are coming from. After working a year with this company I was thrilled to get a promotion. Now it seems like we can't offer young people enough money to assume any type of leadership role."

The tension in the convention room quickly heightened, particularly at a table off to our right full of employees dubbed "kids." We knew that the issue the older members of this large organization had raised was critical, but to summarize the bottom-line of this complicated problem in the remaining thirty minutes seemed impossible.

"Well, to be quite honest with you, what you've all just shared is the natural conflict of having four generations at work in your organization," we began.

> Many of today's companies have four generational groups in the workplace.

Many of today's companies have four generational groups in the workplace. Each generation has distinct characteristics, often very different from the others. In fact, motivation and rewards are just some of the diverse aspects of the Silent Generation, Baby Boomers, Gen Xers, and Millennials.

Needless to say, the final half hour we spent with this group of one hundred and forty leaders from all over the United States was eventful. We quickly summarized the key points which we will guide you through in upcoming sections, discovering that many of these executives had little or no knowledge of the basic differences between the generations in their companies or how this generational diversity was impacting their daily operations.

> These executives had little or no knowledge of the basic differences between the generations in their companies or how this generational diversity was impacting their daily operations.

The best synopsis to that particular seminar surprisingly came from a young man name Jake Olsen who was seated at the table of GenXers. He asked us if he could share about his generation with the rest of the audience members, and we happily handed over the microphone.

"Look," Jake started bluntly (which is typical for members of his generation), "it's not that we don't appreciate our jobs and hope to do well, but we don't want to slave away at our desks and miss out on life either. Actually, most of us really want to connect more, so rather than offering us more incentives, why don't you try to invest in getting to know us better and do more fun things that include everyone at work."

You could have heard a pin drop after Jake's short speech. For the first time in many of these leaders' professional careers, they caught a glimpse of what is on the other side of the gap between themselves and younger team members.

GENERATION GAPS IN THE WORKPLACE

If you can relate to Bud, Hank, and Judy's concerns, you're not alone. Leaders in industries across America have been complaining about similar dilemmas within their corporate families. "What's the matter with these young people? Why don't they have a work ethic like we do? How come no one wants to attend the leadership seminar we're having?'

All of these questions might be summed up as George Coe did in the quote above: "*What ails the youth of today?*" Coe wrote those words in 1925—the senior members of society back in the early 20th century were as concerned then as we are now about the changes in the younger generation. Was it, as some critics of that day pointed out, a result of the "seeds" that were planted simply by being a part of Western civilization? Were the youth being corrupted as technology advanced, values shifted, and ways of life changed? "Or, perhaps does increase of liberty bring into the open certain sorts of conduct that always were either unobtrusively present or else prevented by repression?" (Coe, 1925, p. x).

Even the increase of freedom for young people was thought to be part of the rise in generational problems during that time period. Does this sound familiar? What do we often hear others saying about junior team members, new employees, and interns?

Many complain about how undisciplined they are, how they lack responsibility, and how they don't have a good enough work ethic. And, if we are honest, we're probably not completely innocent, either.

> What's even more amazing is that many senior staff members said similar things about us when we were first hired! The times may have changed, but many of the issues haven't.

What's even more amazing is that many senior staff members said similar things about us when we were first hired! The times may have changed, but many of the issues haven't.

The reality is that our businesses and organizations are complex, richly diverse places that transform with each generation of employees. This enhances the uniqueness of organizations, but it can also add to already existing challenges. As Zemke, Raines, and Filipczak point out, "there is a growing realization that the gulf of misunderstanding and resentment between older, not so old, and younger employees in the workplace is growing and problematic" (2000, p. 1). Unless you, the leader, assume the responsibility for understanding that this gulf is very real and then develop the appropriate skills to help bridge these gaps, the conflicts will only increase in the days ahead.

If you don't, this gulf can become wide, distancing employees from one another. Rather than deal with the alienation, some team members simply leave. Others who stay are often unsatisfied and unfulfilled in their roles, and the discontent is felt strongly by co-workers and clients alike.

In her book, *Connecting Generations: The Sourcebook for a New Workplace*, Raines (2003) explains that there are four generations currently interacting in organizations today. These include the Silent Generation (those born between 1924 and 1945), Baby Boomers (1946–1964), Gen Xers (1965–1980), and Millennials (1981–2000). While researchers have a few different names for some of these generations, most experts agree that there are many similarities between people who fall into these age groups. The commonalities begin from birth as we are "programmed–coded with data about what's right and wrong, good and bad, stylish and geeky, funny and not. As infants, we begin a series of programming experiences that create the filters through which we see the world—especially the world of work—for the rest of our lives" (Raines, 2003, p. 10).

As we move into Part III of *The Leading Edge*, our goal is to guide you beyond where most leadership development programs take you and your High Performance Team. The first of our Team Strategies will assist you through the sometimes murky waters of generational differences, clarifying the types of players you have on your HPT and all throughout your corporate family. We plan to give you very specific strategies to improve your interactions with these four generations of workers; skills that you can also cascade throughout your entire organization. Most importantly, our goal is to assist you in a new role as **Cultural Translator**, someone who competently speaks to each generation and between generations. Refining your approach to this aspect of modern-day leadership will improve your performance in all aspects of life for years to come, no matter what generation you meet along life's journey.

> Our goal is to assist you in a new role as Cultural Translator, someone who competently speaks to each generation and between generations.

THE SILENT GENERATION

During his college years, our youngest son, Jared, began to intern with us during his summer breaks. One of his first assignments was to attend a conference held at a seaside resort where LEADon would serve as keynote speaker for the opening session of a corporate event. As a Millennial, Jared was excited about the event because he would be joining us at beautiful setting filled with new adventure. As Baby Boomers, we were hopeful that he would glean new insights into our business and appreciate the opportunities that lay ahead of him.

The conference was being held for the Academy members of a large professional organization; they had invited their Hall of Fame players from all over the United States. Interestingly, the demographics of this group included five generations because several Academy members were from the Greatest Generation (those born between 1900 and 1924). As over two hundred people took their seats at the round tables, Jared stood in the back, surveying the scene. Just before the organizer of the event introduced us, we noticed several older gentlemen enter the room next to where Jared was standing. He handed them some materials and directed them to an empty table, and then he sat down and began talking with them.

Like we typically do with most groups, we got the table members involved in a rapport builder shortly after our initial remarks. As anxious Baby Boomer parents, we had to check on Jared; we were happy to observe him still engaged with the Greatest Generation and Silent Generation members at his table. Later when we stopped by to talk to the group during a break, these Academy members couldn't wait to tell us how impressed they were with our son. It turns out that during the rapport builder, Jared and these men had entered into a lengthy discussion about a favorite movie star—John Wayne. They loved it! Not only were they pleased to discover that someone from the younger generation actually knew who John Wayne was, but they were thrilled that Jared was able to discuss several of his movies with them.

What Jared was able to accomplish in a very short time is exactly what we hope to pass on to you as leaders of multiple generations. He was able to bond with virtual strangers because these very different generational groups (19 to 90 year-olds) found common ground.

Common ground isn't always easy to find, especially when we're considering the oldest group still active in the workplace, those of the Silent Generation. Some researchers call men and women born from 1924–1945 the "Builder Generation" (Hicks & Hicks, 1999; Raines, 2003). Others refer to them as the Sandwich Generation because they were "sandwiched" between the Greatest Generation and the Boomers (Zemke, Raines, & Filipczak, 2000). Others refer to them as the Traditionalists (Lancaster & Stillman, 2002). No matter what they're labeled, they represent the senior members of our organizations who are nearing retirement but still remain actively engaged in daily operations.

These Silent Generation members came after the Greatest Generation (also called the GI Generation because they served in WWI and/or WWII), but they were highly influenced by them (Hicks and Hicks, 1999). They were builders in the sense that they helped the Greatest Generation reshape American society and the economy after the war. Indeed, some of these Silent Generation members may have founded or helped build the organization you work in today.

Some key characteristics of these members of your corporate family include practicality, dedication, respect, sacrifice, and emphasis on civic responsibility (Raines, 2003). Because of their unique positioning between two large, successful generational groups, these men and women "learned valuable skills in in-between land. Nobody can 'get along' quite the way they do" (Zemke, Raines, Filipczak, 2000, p. 36) As a group, this means that they tend to be good communicators who serve well as mediators because they are fair and "consider the common good" (Raines, 2003, p. 20).

These senior co-workers in our organizations can be viewed by some colleagues as stubborn and refusing to adjust, stuck in the past, or even too old to change. In one company we worked with, a C-level executive complained to us off-line that everyone on staff felt that the president of the company needed to retire and let someone else take over operations. No one could convince him to go, not even his wife, who was eager to travel and enjoy more time with their grandkids. When we finally had a chance, we carefully broached this subject with the president himself. His answer: "I'm not leaving until those so-called leaders on my team are ready to take this company over. I won't let all my hard work go down the drain."

> The Silent Generation members are builders, and they don't want to see what they've worked hard to construct be damaged or destroyed in any way.

This type of response is typical for those who belong to this generation. After all, the Silent Generation members are builders, and they don't want to see what they've worked hard to construct be damaged or destroyed in any way. They've dedicated themselves to their careers, so they are more than willing to sacrifice a little longer before they retire if that is what's needed. Both Bud and Hank from our opening story are from this demographic group. As they expressed, they were struggling with the gap between their generation and the younger employees in their respective organizations, and they didn't want to retire with such an uneasy feeling about those differences.

If you're a member of the Silent Generation, then you are in a good place in this book. The straight line strategies we've already covered should help you pass on to your High Performance Team members those skill sets that will allow them to continue on without you when you're ready to retire. By reading this chapter, you will also be able to help Baby Boomers, Gen Xers, and Millennials understand their respective group characteristics and how they can work together more effectively and efficiently, so that you can be confident that your business will continue to thrive, even without you there anymore.

If you're a member of one of the three other generational groups who still have members of the Silent Generation in your organizations, then don't let their wisdom and expertise go to waste! Take time to discover what they already know, and be sure to include them in current content and information exchanges. Glean all of the history that these "storytellers" and "priests" of your corporate culture hold in their memories. As Deal and Kennedy point out, "storytellers preserve institutions and their values by imparting legends of the company to new employees" while priests are older colleagues who "are the designated worriers of the corporation and the guardians of the culture's values" (1982, pp. 87, 88).

BABY BOOMERS

This group of Americans, born between 1946 and 1964, earned the "boomer" name by surprising statisticians with their explosive population. After WWII, census experts noted the upsurge in births and estimated that 5 million babies would be born by the end of the decade. "How wrong they were! In 1948 the nation's mothers gave birth to 4 million babies—a child was born every eight seconds. By the end of the decade, 9 million babies had been born" (Gillon, 2004, p. 1). And these babies kept coming. In the span of those eighteen years, Baby Boomers would grow to an unprecedented 78 million strong (How Generations Work, July 2009).

> But Baby Boomers also brought to their world a new optimism and a driving work ethic that was passed on by their mothers and fathers who had survived the Great Depression and WWII.

The profound impact of this generational group upon America wasn't only due to its sheer size but also to the changes that occurred as they began to grow up in a rapidly advancing society. The influence of new methods of childrearing, television, and educational opportunities created the generation gap of the 1960s and 1970s (Hicks & Hicks, 1999). Parents and society as a whole felt the distance widening between their values and experiences and those of the younger generation.

But Baby Boomers also brought to their world a new optimism and a driving work ethic that was passed on by their mothers and fathers who had survived the Great Depression and WWII. Because they struggled with authority, they bent the rules and made new ones. And due to their great numbers, they were accustomed to groups and worked as team members. As a whole they believed they could change the world, and they did (Raines, 2003).

In *Boomer Nation: The Largest and Richest Generation Ever and How It Changed America*, a revealing quote sums up this influential segment of the workforce: "The Boomer generation was the first to realize the American dream of equal opportunity for all its citizens...they are passing on to their children a society that is even more open, dynamic, energetic, and innovative" (Gillon, 2004, p. 12). Remember Judy from our opening story? As a Baby Boomer, she was able to ride the wave of opportunity that opened up for women during this transitional time in the United States. As the Vice President at her company, she struggled to understand the younger generations' work ethic compared to those of her fellow Baby Boomers. After speaking to her further, we realized that Judy was interested in new generational ideas and wanted to incorporate better ways of dealing with the GenXers and Millennials in her company.

Baby Boomers, especially those born during the second half of their nineteen-year span, have a strong drive to experience the good life offered to them. They became terrific consumers, and marketing capitalized on this drive. "Their attention continued to be centered on themselves—what they believed to be right, what they wanted, what was good for them" (Hicks & Hicks, 1999). This shift from being problem-solvers to personally-focused confounded many in society, including the younger Gen Xers watching them.

The overall achievements of the Baby Boom Generation have been amazing, but they also came at a price. The driving work ethic caused Boomers to put in long hours on weekdays, and sometimes even longer ones on weekends, to achieve their dreams. Families suffered as a result of these long hours away, ultimately resulting in divorce for some and distance in others. But, many Boomers are now the leaders in organizations across America. Ironically, they now have "the power after rebelling against it for so long" (Gillion, 1994, p. 297).

Since some of the first Baby Boomers are now in their sixties, they are the ones who are retiring or at least considering the possibility of passing on the reins of their organizations to the next generation of leaders. This won't be an easy task for this exceptional group because they've striven so long for success, and they've given much of themselves to improving their world. If you're a leader from this Baby Boom Generation, consider how that "programming" we discussed earlier has impacted you, especially when it comes to your personal and professional life. Your strong work ethic may drive you, but is it driving others around you crazy? Can you find life balance despite your generation's natural craving to change the world (review Chapter 4)? How will you pass on your strong sense of values to younger generations?

We often urge the Boomers in organizations to step back from their leadership roles and look at the overall demographics of their corporate family members. Being part of such a large, powerful demographic can color our perspectives. While some of us still have members of the Silent Generation in the workforce, their numbers are dwindling, and Gen Xers and Millennials will need our full attention if we plan to pass the baton of leadership on to them. This must be an *internal* and *intentional* effort on our parts to understand each other, or the next generation gap in our organizations may be far wider than ever imagined.

If you're reading this section as a member of another demographic, you may be nodding your head thinking, "Yep, this is a perfect description of those Boomers. They've been running the show for a long time—and it's about time they step aside and let us have our shot!" We'd like to re-assure you that your time is coming. So, may this become a time of advanced preparation for you. Use the skill sets that we've been sharing in *The Leading Edge* to glean as much as you can from the Baby Boom Generation in your business. After all, they have established many of the core values that your company now aspires to and laid the groundwork for future potential and profitability. Most of all, catch the spirit of optimism that Boomers possess because it can carry you a long way in your personal and professional journey.

GEN XERS

The fact that Jake Olsen had no problem being direct with that group of high-powered executives we mentioned at the beginning of the chapter doesn't surprise anyone who is familiar with the members of Generation X. Many from this demographic have been waiting their turn to take over for years. As generational expert Gillon points out, "Generation X rejoiced that their parents were losing their grip on the nation's popular culture" (2004, p. 262). Yet, can we blame them when the older generation tells them that "they're soft. They don't know how good they have it. Not only did they never have to fight in a war...they never even had to dodge one" (Gillon, 2003, p. 163)?

Part of Gen Xers' angst may also be attributed to the fact that they were born in the shadow of so many Boomers. Their generational group is roughly half the size of Boomers, and they are sandwiched in between another large demographic, the Millennials. According to some generational experts, "it's a generation that no one ever really noticed, that didn't exactly register, until recently" (Zemke, Raines & Filipczak, 2000, p. 93). For a season, this group was lost in the shuffle like the middle child in a large family; now Gen Xers are positioned in leadership roles and are poised to begin running their organizations.

Those born between 1965 and 1980 have come into their own, personally and professionally. They're raising the next generation of citizens and are actively involved in the workplace as well as the community at large. Indeed, it is their outside interests (and Gen Xers have many of them) that cause some of the conflict in the workplace. Men and women who belong to Generation X are "not out to change the world, just to have a life" (Raines, 2003, p. 15). This clash of values alone exacerbates many of the problems between Boomers and Xers in companies across America; in fact, the clash between these two demographics represents the biggest area of concern for many leaders.

But where did this "life, then work" balance come from? "They grew up in difficult financial times. They were being raised when the traditional family in America was deteriorating, but they held on" (Hicks & Hicks, 1999, p. 254). Many members of Generation X grew up in challenging times and changing home environments. They were often on their own as latch key kids while parents worked. This made them feel disillusioned and abandoned; thus, they chose to be extremely independent. So, in a sense, Xers have a "survival mentality," often not knowing exactly who to trust, except themselves (Zemke, Raines, & Filipczak, 2000, p. 95).

> Xers are quite independent in their work environments.

> Gen Xers also like to keep moving forward.

As a result, Xers are quite independent in their work environments. Unlike their Boomer colleagues who tend to be team players, employees from this demographic group are self-reliant and competent. They know what it takes to get through tough times; in fact, they tend to expect them. Gen Xers also like to keep moving forward, and "they can't stand the thought of reaching a dead end. Their greatest fear is that they might become stagnant" (Lancaster & Stillman, 2002, p. 85).

Generation X's mistrust of the establishment can lead to an immediate search for new employment when problems arise in their organizations; therefore, they mentally prepare to have portable careers. This is part of the reason members of the Silent and Baby Boom Generations often view them as unstable, unreliable, and disloyal (Lancaster & Stilman, 2002). Even though Gen Xers want to move up in their companies, the older members of the corporate family aren't sure they can trust them with new levels of leadership. When Xers leave because they feel they have no more opportunities at the current organization, this only confirms leadership's fears. Thus, a negative cycle has been formed between these generations which must be resolved.

One company that had been struggling with these generational difficulties contacted us about five years ago. The CEO, Jon Wiley, happened to be born during the first year of "the Boom." Nearing retirement, he was extremely concerned about the constant conflict between older and younger staff members. He hadn't realized that many of the issues, especially between leadership and their subordinates, had to do with generational differences. The only thing he knew was that the executive team didn't want any of the junior team members to receive training for leadership; they believed it would be counterproductive since these "flaky" employees would probably leave soon, anyway.

We worked with Jon and his executive team through a series of meetings to increase their awareness of generational differences, and we gave them new strategies on how to interact with the Gen Xers who needed to be trained and equipped for leadership roles. We asked them to build on the positive qualities of this generation, including their ability to work independently, their comfort level with change, and their flexibility.

Many of the Boomers in leadership hadn't noticed how Xers were not only flexible but also very sensitive to people (an asset developed through their own personal struggles while growing up). Needless to say, it didn't take long for constructive changes to take place in this company, including all of the staff members feeling like they were part of a true corporate family.

If you're a member of Generation X, take some time now to think about how your background and experiences have impacted your personal and professional life. How have divorce, economic instability, and transition influenced your views about others? Although you may prefer to work independently, are there ways that this could create problems in your company? Though you know that your "work to live, not live to work" philosophy helps you keep balance, will you understand why it may cause concern for others who don't share this value?

For those of us who are working with Xers (and we're especially talking to those from the Baby Boom Generation), think about some of the issues that have created conflict in your workplace environment. Could it be that you've been so focused on judging and making decisions as you were "programmed" to that you haven't opened up to the idea that these younger members of your corporate family are different for very legitimate reasons? If so, how can you improve your perspective and become more inclusive of those who are "different?"

Indeed, their ability to accept change and differences may be one of the greatest gifts Generation X can pass on to others. "Diversity is a key fact of life for Xers, the core of the perspective they bring…[it] is a hallmark of this generation, a diversity accessible to everyone" (Smith & Churman, 1998, pp. 88–89). Utilize Gen Xers openness and acceptance in your organization, and you may discover that you'll transform in some essential ways as well.

MILLENNIALS

"I can't tell you how difficult it is keeping kids in jobs these days," Tricia Kaplan complained, "that is, if they show up to work at all! We've hired dozens for our stores this past summer and only a handful have remained. Now I've got to go through all of these new applications, and I'm not very confident any of them will be around a year from now if I do hire them."

Tricia, a Baby Boomer who owns and operates a small chain of retail stores, shared that this dilemma wasn't unique to her organization. Many other store owners she knew also had complaints about their younger employees' and interns' lack of commitment to their jobs as well as their constant social networking while on the job.

"I thought the problem was simply because I was in retail," Tricia added, "but my husband's software company is experiencing the same types of problems. The kids there want to get a pay raise almost as soon as they start working, and if you don't reward their efforts, they think you're unhappy with them."

Welcome to the world of Generation Next—or should we say Net—or maybe Gen Y, iGeneration, Echo Boomers, or Millennials. Confused? Join the crowd! There are so many names for members of this demographic born between 1981 and 2000 that it's enough to confound experts in the field. We've decided to utilize the term Millennials since it is used most in generational literature.

Millennials may have acquired all of these names because this group of young people are still finding themselves. Some are entering the workforce as interns or entry level employees, but many are still finishing their education and preparing for adulthood. No doubt the events of September 11th, 2001 as well as the economic crisis of 2008–2009 have influenced and will influence the perspectives and "programming" of this group of 95 million (Raines, 2003; How Generations Work, July 2009).

Though they are young, there are already some key characteristics that describe this large group of Millennials. Probably the most noticeable is how connected they are—thus the "Net" descriptor—due to their exposure to the Internet as well as other technologies. Generational researchers explain that these "kids view technology as just another part of their environment, and they soak it up along with everything else. For many kids, using the new technology is as natural as breathing" (Tapscott, 1999, p. 40). The Millenials have technology at the foundation of everything they do, and they'll want to incorporate it into their professional and personal lives. From texting to blogging to "twittering," Millennials will always be on the cutting edge of telecommunication.

Unfortunately for less-techie Boomers, this can be an area of conflict in the workplace, whereas Gen Xers and Millennials tend to have the area of technology in common. Millennials thrive on what is new and "next" in technology, and they're great multi-taskers who can listen to music, browse a website, text a message, and answer the phone without blinking. It's vital that companies understand these new operating modalities or else they may find themselves "standing on the edge of a generation gap wider than their worst nightmares" (Zemke, Raines, & Filipczak, 2000, p. 129).

> Millennials are a well-educated, open-minded, independent, and caring group.

Millennials are a well-educated, open-minded, independent, and caring group. In part, they have become this way because they were reared by a high-powered generation of Baby

Boomers and family-focused Generation Xers that some say "coddled this generation by constantly telling them how special they were and that anything they sought was possible" (How Generations Work, July 2009). Their soccer moms and dads—also sometimes called "helicopter parents—" rewarded them with praise as well as tangible gifts and their teachers and coaches gave them awards and trophies for just about everything. Basically, Millennials have been reared with the belief that they are exceptional human beings (Raines, 2003).

This perception of uniqueness, enhanced by tremendous amounts of positive reinforcement, makes transitioning into today's workplace far more difficult for Millennials than any other demographic. Most of our organizations are not geared toward protecting, praising, and rapidly promoting our employees, but this is exactly what these members of the younger generation have grown accustomed to in their homes, schools, and communities. Unfortunately, this distinction also translates into a desire for a company phone, computer, and even a car—often on the first day at work. Millennials tend to expect to immediately receive the same perks that previous generations had to wait years to attain.

> This perception of uniqueness, enhanced by tremendous amounts of positive reinforcement, makes transitioning into today's workplace far more difficult for Millennials than any other demographic.

For leaders, this only emphasizes the need for creating a Culture of Appreciation (discussed in detail in Chapter 7) in order to adequately prepare for this generation of workers. While leadership teams certainly should never "coddle" anyone in the corporate family, they must adjust to the reality of how future employees will be motivated and encouraged to work at peak levels of performance. After all, we can't ignore a group that's 95 million strong for very long.

Millennials are also "the most tolerant of all the generations. This, too, is part of their upbringing. This generation has been reared without absolutes. It's perfectly acceptable in elementary school classrooms for there to be more than one right answer to a question" (Zemke, Raines, & Filipczak, 2000, p. 138). Their capacity for tolerance includes their sensitivity to other people, cultures, and ideas. Multiculturalism is important to them, and so is taking care of larger global issues, such as AIDS and poverty.

Having reared two Millennials, we can relate to this passion for serving the community as well as pursuing social issues. Our oldest son, Ryan, hopes to use his medical training with people in poverty-stricken areas both inside and outside of the United States. Another Millennial we know, the twenty-one year old daughter of a successful business man, wants to serve the underprivileged abroad. Instead of rushing off to graduate school (as many of us Boomers would have done so we could get ahead in our professions), Justine is considering taking a year off to travel to developing nations in order to help those in need.

But all of the Millennials' current endeavors and potential opportunities cause them to be a bit restless. In fact, "futurists predict that Millennials will experience as many as ten career changes in their lifetimes. That's *career* changes, not job changes—meaning they will recycle their skills and talents and personal preferences into new applications again and again" (Lancaster & Stillman, 2002, p. 66). In a changing economy, this can be a tremendous benefit to some businesses, but it's worrisome to others, especially those that invest heavily in training and equipping their corporate family members.

Thus, Millennials have been dubbed the generation that will be seeking "parallel" careers.

As a leader, you must prepare to meet this next generation of workers head on. "It's not going to be business as usual. This group has a strong self-image. They feel confident in the abilities they bring" (Hicks & Hicks, 1999, p. 281). Their potential strengths are numerous, including their positive attitude toward work, like the Silent Generation, the teamwork capabilities of Boomers, and the technological skill sets of Gen Xers (Zemke, Raines & Filipczak, 2000). But, they will need lots of guidance and support, not only because they're chronologically young but also because they're accustomed to a hands-on approach, similar to the one they experienced in their family units. The coaching and mentoring process that you've been integrating with your HPT (recall this discussion in Chapter 7?) will be especially useful as you and your colleagues interact with Millennials.

If you are a Millennnial, we're confident that many of you will be assuming roles of leadership in the not-too-distant future. We urge you, as we have the other generations, to step back and carefully analyze why you interact in your world the way that you do. Your demographic is indeed unique, in part because of the technological advances that you've been exposed to since birth. But, please realize that you are not alone in this specialness. Each of the generational groups you are currently working with, as well as those that will follow you, have distinct characteristics that add a richness and diversity to your organization and your life as a whole. Embrace them as well as the straight line strategies we've been discussing. They will not only help you reach your optimum potential, but they'll also prepare you to work with the generations that will follow in your own personal and professional journey.

BECOMING A CULTURAL TRANSLATOR

Several years ago we witnessed a very interesting scene. An elderly woman stood at a counter of a New York department store holding several items. She stared blankly at the male clerk who was asking if she needed help. Finally the lady spoke—but in Italian. The clerk quickly said, "Oh, I'm sorry, I only speak English."

The elderly lady pointed at an item, obviously trying to communicate something in Italian. Once again the young clerk responded, "I wish I could help you, but I don't know what you're asking."

Fortunately the department manager, who was just finishing up with another customer, moved to the counter to see if she could be of assistance. It turned out that this manager spoke Spanish, which, for the elderly woman, was close enough. They began an animated verbal exchange of questions and answers, and the issue—which happened to be finding a garment in a different size—was resolved.

This department store manager did exactly what we're hoping you will be able to accomplish in your organization. We want you to become a translator in your work environment! Translation skills won't be only about the "language" that your corporate family members are speaking. You will also have to become fluent in the different cultures of the generations in your care.

You've already started the process of becoming a **Cultural Translator** by beginning to research and understand the generational differences you may face. To further build on your knowledge, let's look at translation's three basic steps:

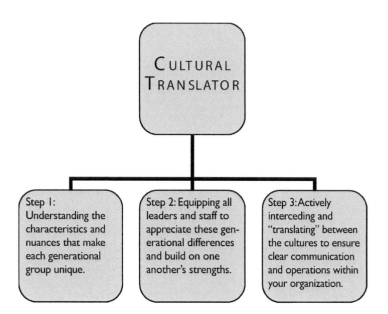

As you've already observed, the four generations working in your company are unique. They are diverse in background, experiences, values, current philosophies, and future plans. Those in the Silent Generation wanted to build "lifetime careers," which explains why many of them still aren't ready to leave. Boomers are looking for "stellar careers" that make a difference, while Gen Xers are thinking about "portable" ones because they're not sure how long the organization will last. Finally, those Millennials are planning "parallel" futures with lots of options (Lancaster & Stillman, 2002). And we wonder why we have so much trouble understanding one another in our companies!

> As a leader, you must be able to understand these differences as well as assist your corporate family members in gaining these new perspectives.

As a leader, you must be able to understand these differences as well as assist your corporate family members in gaining these new perspectives. "Leading in a culture of change is about unlocking the mysteries of living organizations" (Fullan, 2001, p. 46). Your company is comprised of living beings, not just products and processes, and some of the greatest mysteries yet to be uncovered in many companies across this county include how the diverse generations impact day-to-day operations.

This is not to say that equipping your HPT in generational issues will solve all of your problems. "Not every organizational problem, foul-up, shortcoming, and faux pas has a cross-generational origin...but when you do have a cross-generational problem, you know it. It can permeate everything that goes wrong" (Zemke, Raines, & Filipczak, 2000, p. 213). When you address this one critical area, how much easier will it be for your HPT to resolve other dilemmas? If all four generations of your corporate family are relating to one another well, then they will be able to implement positive skills sets to help resolve whatever problems are at hand without any of their differences getting in the way.

We realize it will probably be easier for you to accomplish step one of this process than the second, because it can be much more complex as it requires *internal* and *intentional* effort with and within your HPT. Equipping your corporate family members with translation skills is a time-intensive effort—time you may not feel you have on many days. Leaders often require assistance to attain expertise in new areas, just as they may need help equipping team members with the skills needed to transform over time, so don't despair with the struggles you're having in cultural translation.

However you choose to engage your employees, realize that the more you do to encourage these cultural changes the better.

"All successful organizations in a culture of change have been found...to seek diversity of employees, ideas, and experiences while simultaneously establishing mechanisms for sorting out, reconciling, and acting on new patterns" (Fullan, 2001, p. 75). Here are a few ideas for you to begin improving generational understanding in your corporate family:

+ Hold a Generational Awareness Week. Start with a workshop and then practice new strategies during that week.
+ Ask employees from the four generations to come up with three rewards specific to each generation.
+ Allow employees to examine a company problem from different angles, specifically from generational perspectives other than their own.
+ Have groups write your core values according to how the different generations would apply them.
+ Design your employment application for different generations, especially the Millennials. Be sure to include questions that hone in on their potential strengths.

> Leaders of today and tomorrow must be able to assist their High Performance Teams and organizations to motivate, incentivize, and lead the various generations interacting in the workplace.

This concept of becoming a Cultural Translator has been batted about the halls of academia for some time, but its implementation into the corporate world is vital in the times in which we live. Leaders of today and tomorrow must be able to assist their High Performance Teams and organizations to motivate, incentivize, and lead the various generations interacting in the workplace, especially because "the future holds promise for strong culture companies. Strong cultures are not only able to respond to an environment, but they also adapt to diverse and changing circumstances" (Deal & Kennedy, 1982, p. 195).

Remember also, this must be a team effort. You will only be able to serve as a Cultural Translator for a season; after that, it will be up to those leaders that you are training—your HPT—to be able to implement and pass these skill sets on to the next generation of leaders. They will be guided from your role-modeling, and they will learn from the training opportunities you offer them. Best of all, each of the generations will learn how to work together to compete for the leading edge as they realize cultural translation's lifelong benefits for them, as well as for those who will one day follow in their footsteps.

SHARPENING YOUR EDGE

1. To which generational group do you belong? How do you identify with the characteristics of your generation? How have generational differences impacted you, your team, and your organization?

2. Analyze your organizational chart and figure out how many employees fall into each of the four generational groups. Develop a plan based on the strategies in this chapter to encourage rapport and communication in and between the generations during the next month.

3. Will the process of evaluating fellow team members change now that you know each of them belongs to a specific generation? How do the differences in generational groups impact your reviews of team members and future business plans?

4. Become a Cultural Translator! Choose one of the books we've referenced in this chapter. Read it during the next month, then share your new insights with your team members from all generations.

Chapter **N I N E**

Corporate Culture Always Impacts the Bottom Line

The great law of culture is: Let each become all that he was created capable of being.

Thomas Carlyle

I n the previous chapter we introduced the concept of "Cultural Translator" and explained how your ability to serve in this role will dramatically improve the interactions between your employees from different generations. While enhancing communication and improving the relationships of your colleagues and staff are essential goals for you as a leader, leaders also must maximize the work environment so that everyone can operate at optimum levels of performance.

The next level of exceptional leadership is ***creating a profitable and productive Corporate Culture.*** Once again, we are striving to set high expectations and let you dive deeper into the leadership process, thinking about the bigger picture in your organization by studying its unique nuances, idiosyncrasies, and possibilities. As we continue in Part III, our goal is to hone your ability to develop Team Strategies that won't just make a difference today but will leave a legacy long after you are gone.

Defining culture isn't an easy task. Anthropologists and sociologists have struggled for years to find a clear-cut explanation of this very complex concept (Garcia, 2002). One of the oldest explanations we found states that culture is, "the sum and substance of the thoughts and beliefs of a people" (Wissler, 1923, p. 3). Benedict defined culture as, "what really binds men together...the ideas and the standards they have in common" (1934, p. 14). *Men and women aren't simply part of a culture—they define culture by the ideas they agree upon or those beliefs they choose to unite around.*

> Men and women aren't simply part of a culture—they define culture by the ideas they agree upon or those beliefs they choose to unite around.

Many would have described culture as a people group somewhere on the globe or perhaps an activity, such as music, art or dance. But culture is about *the commonality of the people,* rather than where they are from or their ancestry. When we look at it in this broader scope, that means you and your team members at work have a culture too. You have "tangible, symbolic, and ideational" characteristics that set you apart from the company across the street or the competitor across town (Banks, 2001, p. 70). As Garcia notes, your employees have a "system of understanding [that] includes values, beliefs, notions about acceptable and unacceptable behavior, and other socially constructed ideas" (2002, p. 73).

> Culture is about the commonality of the people, rather than where they are from or their ancestry.

For example, if we walked into your organization, we would notice some very specific nuances. Your company would have a "feel" to it, and you and your employees would act in unique ways compared to other companies with whom LEADon consults.

Bob Jenkins (from Chapter 5) immediately knew something was different about Designer Graphics as soon as the reception-ist answered the phone. He liked the staff and the president. The atmosphere was professional yet friendly, enhanced by his comparison to the negative attitude of his own secretary. The company slogan was highly visible, even on many employ-ees T-shirts. Designer Graphics appeared to be such a great environment Bob didn't even want to return to his own place of business.

This is a great story for Designer Graphics, but not for Bob's organization. He should have been the most comfortable where he had to spend the majority of his day. Several leaders we talk to are often out of the office because they simply can't stand the attitudes or actions of their co-workers and employees, so they avoid the situation as much as possible. For many, the culture is one of the reasons for contacting a company like LEADon. A recent e-mail from a new client read, "I think we should spend about three hours focusing on some rapport building and talk-ing about our culture." This CEO realized that *culture* is where his organization's leadership development needed to begin in order to start affecting the bottom line.

If you're sensing that your organization may be lacking positive culture, then this chapter is definitely for you. On the other hand, if you feel that you and your HPT have a terrific culture, then we'd like to help you keep it that way. As an exceptional leader, you can readily implement the follow-ing straight line strategies to ensure that a positive Corporate Culture is passed on to the next generation of leaders.

EVERY ORGANIZATION HAS A CULTURE

Before we move any further in this chapter, we want to reassure you that the concept of positive culture is not a soft-science. At first, some of the straight line strategies to success that we've covered seem irrelevant to leaders, in part because they're not typical business approaches. Many of the approaches to exceptional leadership, such as EQ skills and the Culture of Appreciation, are not often addressed in business courses, and they won't have a labeled spot on your Profit and Loss Statement, but they can profoundly impact what you do as an organization on a daily basis.

While forming a positive culture may not seem to fit into your current goals and strategies, we assure you that its impact on your company, colleagues, and clients will be tremendous, and it will be especially noticeable over time. Culture is at the foundation for everything you and your co-workers do. In their landmark book, *Corporate Cultures: The Rites and Rituals of Corporate Life,* Deal and Kennedy explain that "whether weak or strong, culture has a powerful influence…culture also has a major effect on the success of the business" (1982, p. 4).

In our experience, Corporate Culture can be defined by these characteristics:

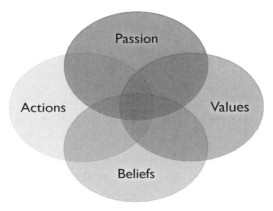

These four characteristics of culture can essentially be divided into two basic components:

1. Passion for the work
2. Three Pillars that support the work—Values, Beliefs and Behavior Patterns

PASSION FOR THE WORK

Many leaders consider the importance of Passion to be an intangible component when we first talk to them about the culture of their companies. We ask executives what kind of atmosphere clients sense when they come to their office, or how their organizations 'feel' to their employees. We suggest that they ask themselves if there is energy, excitement, and enthusiasm for the work their employees are doing, as well. While some men and women have a difficult time answering these types of questions, leadership experts look for these characteristics when they enter organizations as part of their initial assessments. It is important to realize that potential clients go through the same questions as they consider your business.

> Culture is at the foundation for everything you and your co-workers do.

Coyle noted something unique about exceptional companies with great Corporate Culture: in "talent hotbeds, I saw a lot of passion…the feeling wasn't always shiny and happy… but the passion was always there, providing the emotional rocket fuel that keeps them firing their circuits, honing skills, getting better" (2009, pp. 97–98).

This Passion is the glue that binds all aspects of your organization together—from staff to business goals to productivity and profitability. So, how is the level of Passion in your workplace? Are members of your HPT enthusiastic about the work they're doing? Do your corporate family members have a spring in their step because they're excited about getting to the office each day and accomplishing great things together? Ask the same questions of yourself. Is your Passion for the work still as high as it was when you first began? Do you exude Passion so that it creates an air of enthusiasm that is contagious for everyone around you?

> Passion is the glue that binds all aspects of your organization together—from staff to business goals to productivity and profitability.

According to Deal and Kennedy, "the environment in which a company operates determines what it must do to be a success. The business environment is the single greatest influence in shaping a corporate culture" (1982, p. 13). As a leader, it's your ultimate responsibility to create an environment that allows everyone on your High Performance Team to work at their optimum level of potential. This environment must start with you. If you have a poor attitude about your role and responsibilities, this negative mood will be passed on to every employee like a contagious virus. If your offices are shabby, dark, unpleasant places, don't be surprised when your team isn't performing as highly as you had hoped. If you've hired obnoxious, unlikeable hot shots, then don't look any further than yourself to blame for the lack of cooperation on your HPT.

> There is great news when it comes to your Corporate Culture: Cultures should and do change.

However, there is great news when it comes to your Corporate Culture: *Cultures should and do change.* When the company is mediocre, it must change. If the economy has shifted or is struggling, your organization has to adjust. If business is booming or the company is growing rapidly, the culture ought to be willing to expand and grow, too.

But be careful: strong cultures, whether they are good or bad, are extremely difficult to change. Bad ones don't readily transform because they become bogged down and quite comfortable in their state of mediocrity. Good ones—even great ones—may fear that any shift might mess up the system.

> Strong cultures, whether they are good or bad, are extremely difficult to change.

If you truly want to improve the culture of your organization, then you must first carefully analyze what the current status of that culture is and what, if anything, needs to be adjusted right now. If Passion is lacking in your pursuit of productivity and profitability, then re-igniting the fire starts with you. Increase your Passion, and you'll profoundly impact everyone around you. By doing so, you'll be able to improve the culture and ensure that everyone on your team is as excited as you are about what the future holds.

> Increase your Passion, and you'll profoundly impact everyone around you.

CULTURE'S THREE PILLAR APPROACH

As we mentioned above, culture is a complex concept, and there are many definitions to try to explain all of its components. Passion is one piece of the puzzle, but there are three pillars that add support to the work you are doing. These are Values, Beliefs, and Behavior Patterns.

Let's take a look at what each of these three pillars mean:

1. *Values*: the principles, goals, or standards held and accepted by a group of people.
2. *Beliefs:* statements or virtues that people accept as true.
3. *Behavior Patterns:* specific actions that relay general character, state of mind, or response to circumstances.

What you and your co-workers value will be one of the greatest strengths within your Corporate Culture. These core principles not only reflect the character of the company but also that of all employees. In a sense, they represent what you're willing to strive for, sacrifice for, and practically die for. Honesty and integrity are examples of company values that provide strength and structure for the entire business model. When everyone in your organization holds these as values, productivity and profitability can't help but improve. "Values define 'success' in concrete terms for employees—'If you do this, you too will be a success'" (Deal & Kennedy, 1982, p. 14).

> At LEADon, we encourage the process of "memorializing" values in the organizations with which we work.

At LEADon, we encourage the process of "memorializing" values in the organizations with which we work. It's usually easy for leaders to say what they value, but putting it in writing (in a mission statement, for instance) takes deeper thought (Haughton, 2004). You should memorialize your company's goals, objectives, mission statement, core values, and even slogans so they can be shared and reviewed by all employees and potential clients.

This values clarification process strengthens companies. These are the organizations that will thrive in the current marketplace as well as in the future. "Visionary companies are so clear about what they stand for and what they're trying to achieve that they simply don't have room for those unwilling or unable to fit their exacting standards" (Collins & Porras, 1994, p. 9). Exceptional people will stay and those who refuse to accept the current, changing culture will leave.

Beliefs represent a second pillar to successful Corporate Cultures. People in the corporation accept statements of belief about their culture as true much as they would doctrines of faith. For example, Sears has stated for years that it brings "quality at a good price." The employees believed it and sold that concept along with Sears products to consumers. The DuPont Company excelled because they believed in and delivered their logo: "better things for better living" to the public.

A particularly interesting organization is Southwest Airlines. This visionary company explains that "the mission of Southwest Airlines is dedication to the highest quality of Customer Service delivered with a sense of warmth, friendliness, individual pride, and Company Spirit" (www.southwest. com). If you've ever been on one of their flights, there could be no doubt that their employees not only accept this statement as true but also actively demonstrate it on a consistent basis. Perhaps this is why Southwest Airlines was one of five top performing stocks from 1972 to 1992 (Pfeffer, 1995).

Take a few minutes to evaluate what you and your co-workers believe in. Are there unwritten ideas and ideals that you are all striving for? What are the memorialized thoughts and beliefs you uphold as a widely-shared philosophy? Do you have faith that your organization's beliefs are true, or are you and your HPT simply faking it in order to try to stay productive and profitable?

Behavior Patterns will naturally coincide with values and beliefs. They are specific actions which reveal what your organization is really all about. The day-to-day routines of your

> Behavior Patterns are powerfully influenced by the leaders of an organization. Companies with great Corporate Cultures have leaders who understand that they must communicate what is expected of employees.

corporate family members are hugely affected by behavior patterns, but they also affect the ways employees communicate with and relate to others. How employees interact with one another and with clients clearly represents the general character of your corporation. How a High Performance Team responds to various circumstances, particularly in times of crisis, is also crucial to the overall success of your company and its culture. And don't forget those special times of celebration. Your company meetings, get-togethers, and celebrations are all part of your organization's Behavior Patterns.

Behavior Patterns are powerfully influenced by the leaders of an organization. Companies with great Corporate Cultures have leaders who understand that they must communicate what is expected of employees. Standards should have been memorialized for all to see so that, should any question arise about expectations, clarification can be easily obtained by every member of the corporate family. For example, one school district that we worked with not only had a detailed employee handbook for everyone on the payroll, but they also had an unwritten expectation that things would be done "the district's way." Everyone from teachers to administrators diligently strove to act in such a manner that would proudly represent that district, whether at work or in the community.

Can you picture your employees caring enough about your Corporate Culture that on their off-time they wanted to represent it well? Consider if your HPT engages in the types of behaviors that strongly support the overall success of the entire organization. Wouldn't it be wonderful if everyone on your team believed in delivering a "sense of warmth, friendliness, individual pride, and Company Spirit" like the employees of Southwest Airlines?

As a leader, it's ultimately your responsibility to create a culture that encourages Passion in all members of your corporate family and helps to define the Values, Beliefs, and Behavior Patterns everyone should strive to uphold. Your culture will either inspire or alienate—there's no middle ground. Culture defines the environment that you and all employees operate in every day. Since this is true, let's see how you can take these principles and put them into practice.

As a leader, it's ultimately your responsibility to create a culture that encourages Passion in all members of your corporate family and helps to define the Values, Beliefs, and Behavior Patterns everyone should strive to uphold.

DEFINING YOUR CORPORATE CULTURE

Imagine living in a bland community where nothing inspires you. The houses all look alike, the stores sell nothing of interest, and no one ever cared enough to create any landscape or parks. In this insipid community, there is no communication between the people who live there, no common language, no special celebrations, and no shared values. Why would anyone want to stay? How long before you put your house up for sale and move out?

Some employees feel that their organizations are just like this community; that is part of the reason why the retention of high-quality men and women is a challenge for some companies. *By nature, human beings thrive in healthy, engaging, clearly-defined systems—places that provide comfort as well as connection.* Perhaps you've inherited an organization that has a weak or unhealthy cultural history. Well, the good news is you can change it—*you must change it!*

As you continue this process of analyzing your organization, the next step to achieving the leading edge involves actively defining your Corporate Culture. Sometimes this means defining it in real, tangible terms for the very first time in the company's history. In some instances, this may require re-defining the culture in order to keep current with market and societal changes. And, of course, there are the inevitable "complete makeovers" that some companies need to survive at all.

We recommend two specific tactics for defining the culture of your organization:

1. *Find out what aspects of culture are currently working for you and your corporate family, then reinforce these on a regular basis.* For instance, if you've got great core values in place, then talk about them at meetings. Post them up in the conference room. Send positive e-mail messages when you observe someone putting them into practice. Some companies place them on their corporate vehicles, payroll checks, T-shirts, and stationery.

2. *Make a list of what is weak or missing in your company's cultural experiences. Target the most important one and begin to improve it immediately.* Let's say your company hasn't invested much in celebrations—maybe because money is tight. You can still plan a company picnic; just do it the old-fashioned way where everyone brings something for a potluck. Whatever you do, get your corporate family together at different points in the year so they feel and stay connected.

In particular, it's up to you as a leader to ensure that the Three Pillars of your Corporate Culture are clearly defined. Everyone—including you—should be able to explain the Values, Beliefs, and Behavior Patterns that represent your organization. And you and all employees must live out a Passion for the work that you're doing. While the pillars support the organization, your Passion will be the glue that keeps those pillars standing. Be sure that you clearly grasp these concepts, then cascade them to your HPT and everyone else in your corporate family.

> Everyone—including you—should be able to explain the Values, Beliefs, and Behavior Patterns that represent your organization.

As you begin to implement this strategic approach, expect some difficulties along the way. "Change always threatens a culture. People form strong attachments to heroes, legends, the rituals of daily life, the hoopla of extravaganzas…all the symbols and settings of the work place" (Deal & Kennedy, 1982, p. 157). Some employees might be annoyed that you're upsetting the way things have always been done. Others may even be confused or angry because the changes in the culture make them feel insecure.

> If you do so with respect and a degree of sensitivity, you will win more supporters over to your new and improved cultural system than you will adversaries.

Despite the difficulties that you will face in defining or redefining your organization's culture, you must press on. If you do so with respect and a degree of sensitivity, you will win more supporters over to your new and improved cultural system than you will adversaries.

This buy-in will be invaluable to future endeavors. Also, all members of your HPT will be able to operate at peak performance as they begin to thrive, working in an inspiring culture.

BAD CULTURE AND GOOD BUSINESS DON'T MIX

After years of working with many diverse leaders and organizations, we've discovered one important truth: *bad cultures make for bad business.* There are simply no exceptions to this rule. You can't have a mediocre Corporate Culture and do great business. You might find a great culture that struggles from time to time, especially during market fluctuations or in the event of a company crisis, but more than likely this organization will rebound because of the employees' resolve to stick to their Values, Beliefs, and Behavior Patterns. But in a business with a negative culture, leaders aren't happy, and neither is the rest of the staff. And if clients don't like you, they'll find someone else with whom they're more comfortable doing business.

> Bad cultures make for bad business.

Some time ago, LEADon was hired to assist an organization after the board terminated the Chief Executive Officer. This CEO had been in his position for thirty years, and it was past time for his departure. At the time of termination, the board had agreed that this was the best path forward. However after our initial interview with the members of the board, we discovered the following: that they had no plan about how to tell employees about the termination or about how to find a new leader, either from within their organization or outside it.

After a few more indecisive weeks passed, the board began to lose their resolve and fragment. The majority of the board wanted to move forward and redefine the organization in terms of character, roles and responsibilities, vision, mission, and values. Yet even with our attempts at assisting this process, all of their decision-making came to a complete stop. Some members claimed they'd been "coerced" and expressed that the old days might not have been so bad after all. The team members (a term we use loosely for this group) were in such a state of disunion and disagreement that they couldn't make any decisions at all.

> No one can fix an organization except its culture members.

Shortly after our contract with this organization ended, we received word from one of the board members who had originally sought our services that the culture was literally imploding—and revenue was down 45%. Business was still getting done, but it was chaotic at best. Almost everyone on staff was still brewing over the CEO's departure, and no new leader had been chosen to replace him at that point. Since the initial firing of their leader, the company is still floundering. Feedback came to us not long ago that if the organization had implemented our recommendations to improve the Corporate Culture, solutions to three decades of poor leadership would have been remedied.

This is a sad state in which to leave any business, and we certainly tried our best to get the leaders to see that their culture had been destructive and would not get better without internal and intentional effort on everyone's part. *But no one can fix an organization except its culture members.* If the owners of the culture refuse to accept help and don't have the willingness or desire to improve the Corporate Culture, then no one else will be able to lead them through that process, and business will continue to go down.

On the other hand, great cultures stimulate good business. Fortunately, we've observed this in numerous organizations across the country and internationally. One example is an architectural firm that opened a satellite office in another city. This company was founded by several executives who believed Corporate Culture was the basis for the overall success of their business as well as the satisfaction of all their employees. The Passion of employees was evident in both their work and business environment, and clients were drawn to the organization because they quickly observed Passion accompanied by outstanding Values, Beliefs, and Behavior Patterns. Even the new satellite office had taken on the culture despite the distance between the two sites, and its productivity and profitability were on the rise with only six employees in the start-up phase.

> **Great cultures stimulate good business.**

THE BOTTOM LINE

Let's envision this new Corporate Culture you're working on in detail. The environment is attractive, comfortable, and conducive to completing the work you and your co-workers are doing. People trust one another, have realistic expectations, and use "group genius" to get the business goals accomplished. There's an inspiring Passion and energy that clients wouldn't find with any of your competitors. Values and Beliefs are something all members of the corporate family talk about, and there are also Behavior Patterns that reflect those principles. Your HPT and staff members uphold their end of the Corporate Culture, and they insist that everyone else does too.

One pivotal question remains to be answered: Why have you, the leader, gone to all of this trouble in the first place? Is it simply so that you can say, "We've got a great Corporate Culture in our organization." Or is it so everyone feels great about going to work each morning? While both of these are commendable goals, you may feel they really aren't sound reasons in and of themselves for investing all of your time, effort and energy in this process.

Unless, of course, the change is reflected in profitability. Many experts feel that this particular straight line strategy *is* critical to your organization's ultimate success. The productivity and profitability of your business depends on culture, and the culture would be non-existent without your business. They go hand-in-hand in impacting the bottom line!

> The productivity and profitability of your business depends on culture, and the culture would be non-existent without your business. They go hand-in-hand in impacting the bottom line!

Kotter and Heskett conducted a landmark study called *Corporate Culture and Performance* (1992). They looked at 207 large U.S. companies in twenty-two different industries over an eleven-year period. They found that companies that managed their cultures experienced revenue increases of 682% versus 166% for companies that did not manage their cultures well. In addition, stock prices increased 901% versus 74%, with a net increase of 765% versus 1% respectively. Pfeffer (1995) reported on a study of thirty-four large American firms, discovering that a participative culture reaped a Return on Investment (ROI) that averaged nearly *twice as high* as those in firms with less efficient cultures. This study also revealed that there was a strong link between cultural and behavioral aspects of organizations in both their short-term and long-term survival.

A University of Michigan study of over 300 organizations provided empirical evidence of the relationship between a strong Corporate Culture and the bottom line (Denison, 1990). Internationally, the data is consistent—in 1996, the British Institute of Management surveyed executives involved in a number of acquisitions. When those organizations experienced failure, the difficulties in merging two cultures were a major contributing factor (Carleton & Linebeery, 2001).

> As an exceptional leader, you must ensure that your Corporate Culture impacts the bottom line in the most significant ways possible.

While the concept of Corporate Culture may seem intangible to some executives, those who are striving to attain the leading edge in the 21st century are taking a look at how a mix of Passion, Values, Beliefs, and Behavior Patterns might prove to be the path to success. As an exceptional leader, you must ensure that your Corporate Culture impacts the bottom line in the most significant ways possible. Indeed, culture may very well be the variable that your formula for productivity and profitability has been missing.

The author Thomas Carlyle who wrote the quote that started this chapter was fascinated by leadership. In the 19th century his last major work was on the epic life of Frederick the Great, whose leadership helped create a new moral culture during his lifetime. Carlyle pointed out a truth about culture that all leaders should know: *great cultures allow the individual to become the best that he or she can be.* "Your leadership in a culture of change will be judged as effective or ineffective not by who you are as a leader, but by what leadership you produce in others" (Fullan, 2001, p. 137). Passing on the concept of culture is a mandate for leadership, but you cannot, and should not, do it alone. These timeless principles must be handed down to your High Performance Team members so they in turn can equip the next generation of leaders who follow.

Understanding the culture of your corporation is one of the straight line strategies that will help you in this *internal* and *intentional* process toward exceptional leadership. You will become a better leader as you implement these principles, and your HPT will grow stronger in its abilities both now and in the future. As you travel down this new path toward improving your entire team, you will also be building a winning culture that will continue to find success because, as Wissler reminds us, "...tribes may come and tribes may go, but culture goes on forever" (1923, p. 39).

> Passing on the concept of culture is a mandate for leadership.

SHARPENING YOUR EDGE

1. During the next week, walk around your organization and look for the presence or absence of these key pieces to Corporate Culture. Develop a plan that will improve the environment for all corporate family members:
   - Passion
   - Values
   - Beliefs
   - Behavior Patterns

2. Share your findings from #1 with your HPT, and get their feedback on these important issues.

3. How is your passion for the work? How about your team and the rest of your corporate family? Are there ways to re-ignite passion? How will you keep it thriving over time?

4. Create a survey to find out how corporate family members view your Corporate Culture. Ask how your organization compares to other businesses where these employees have worked. Get ideas on how they think the Corporate Culture could be improved.

Leaving a Lasting Legacy through Internal and Intentional Leadership

Having now finished the work assigned me I retire from the great theater of action.

George Washington

Perhaps never before in the history of business has the topic of legacy been of such tremendous importance. Leaders in companies across the United States are talking about how they want to leave a lasting legacy in their organizations. We've discussed the concept with board members in both non-profit and for-profit companies because they have a strong desire to make a difference, and many members of High Performance Teams have shared with us how they want to be certain that the work they're doing will truly last.

This emphasis on leaving something substantial behind or handing down an inheritance for the next generation may in part be a contribution of the Baby Boom Generation (reflect back on Chapter 8) whose ultimate desire has been to change the world. Of course the Gen Xers and Millennials who grew up with these Boomers as role models have also adopted this goal as part of their own generational trademarks. So, it seems that current generations in the workforce are focused on what type of legacy they will leave behind, both personally and professionally.

In the scheme of life, this is an extremely noble ambition. This zest for attaining something better and passing that on to others also fuels productivity and profitability. We've seen this type of aspiration in men and women throughout history and in all aspects of life. From the earliest of civilizations to America, one of the most recent, the historical record reveals the powerful impact that a great legacy can have on people. George Washington is one such example.

> This zest for attaining something better and passing that on to others also fuels productivity and profitability.

After Washington served his country throughout the Revolutionary War, he was ready to retire to his beloved Mount Vernon and resume the life of a civilian. Yet, his fellow countrymen clamored for his return, and he agreed. He served two terms as president, helping to define the fledgling democracy. Historians agree that this nation might not have ever come into existence without Washington's leadership (McCullough, 2001).

George Washington didn't start out wanting to leave a lasting legacy, but there is no doubt about the invaluable inheritance he left behind. Was he perfect? Of course not! In his book *1776*, McCullough describes many of the struggles Washington had in his early days. But he kept going, and he always urged his subordinates to keep their eyes fixed on the ultimate goal of success. Washington seemed to sense that "he was mortal and replaceable…he did what he had to do, then handed the work off to others…" (Brookhiser, 2008, p. 229; 224).

This is the final "straight line strategy" that we want to have you consider as we wrap up this journey to attaining the leading edge: *you can leave a lasting legacy through internal and intentional leadership.* Although you may not be ready to even think about retiring, you must begin preparations for passing all the skill sets you've acquired to the members of your High Performance Team. These are the next line of leaders who will be able to take what you've done and successfully move your organization into the future. A great general, like Washington, prepares his subordinates for leadership because they will need to take command one day. Hall of Fame coaches hire assistant coaches to help and to be ready to lead. So it is with exceptional leaders in thriving organizations—they must equip their colleagues and corporate family members with the skills needed to do the work, today and well into the future.

> Hall of Fame coaches hire assistant coaches to help and to be ready to lead.

Lessons in Legacy

The word legacy has an interesting origin. It comes from the Latin word "lego" which means to ordain, appoint, or bequeath. Either a person or some item was especially designated to be "left behind." For you, the leader, legacy refers to:

1. *Who* you leave behind, personally and professionally, and,
2. *What* you've accomplished, both tangible and intangible.

Let's consider the first aspect of legacy. The "whos" describe those key players in your life, including family, friends, colleagues, and corporate family members. You've spent time equipping individuals in one way or another to become the next generation of leaders. At work, these men and women should be easily identifiable in your HPT. While they may not take over your specific role in the organization, they should be quite capable of assisting whoever does assume that position in the future. These co-workers ought to be able to pass on your mission, vision, core values, and business strategies to future generations of employees. They can do so if they've been mentored in all of the skill sets and "straight line strategies" needed to complete these essential tasks.

> This means much more than hand-picking someone to take your place; instead it's about equipping your entire team to successfully move the organization into the future.

Thus, when we discuss the "who" of your legacy, we're really talking about succession planning on the grandest scale. This means much more than hand-picking someone to take your place; instead it's about equipping your entire team to successfully move the organization into the future. This type of succession planning is about the ultimate well-being of the entire corporate family. "It's perhaps best understood as any effort designed to ensure the continued effective performance of an organization...by making provision for the development, replacement, and strategic application of key people over time" (Rothwell, 2009, pp. 5–6).

As you look back on all that you've accomplished with your HPT, think about the strategic approaches that you've already been implementing. Are members of your HPT learning these skill sets? How are they doing at cascading them down to their subordinates? What areas do they still need to improve on? How can this be accomplished in the upcoming weeks, months, and years of your tenure?

Remember, passing on leadership skills to your High Performance Team is a process. Like any journey in life, it takes time. Some of the pathways to success may be quicker based on the talents and expertise of your team, and others may be more arduous due to a long history of negative attributes or unhealthy patterns that must be removed and replaced. *All that you are doing to attain the leading edge for yourself and your corporate family will pay off down the road, including your efforts at leaving a legacy of people rather than products or profits.* "The reinvention in succession management as a mechanism for identifying and cultivating leadership has occurred only in the last several years, [and] a few farsighted firms…realized the power and potential of succession planning systems that were well aligned with other aspects of leadership development" (Fulmer & Conger, 2004, p. 6).

> All that you are doing to attain the leading edge for yourself and your corporate family will pay off down the road, including your efforts at leaving a legacy of people rather than products or profits.

The second valuable piece to leaving a lasting legacy is the "what" of your work. Notice that we defined this as both a tangible and intangible concept. Let's start with the easier part: the tangible. This is the bottom line result of your life's work. On a personal level, this includes your home, financial assets, collections, and other concrete representations about what's important to you. Your professional legacy consists of the work that you've accomplished over the years—a particular product, the development of a company, or a change you inspired in your industry. You may have designed plans, written books, earned awards, or constructed buildings. These physical examples of your productivity will also carry on after your journey on Earth has come to an end. Which of these tangible aspects of your legacy are you most proud of? How do you want people to view them throughout time? What do you still hope to accomplish?

> This personal legacy of what you believed in represents the essence of who you really are. You have impacted individuals with your ideals, hopes, dreams, values, beliefs, and behavior patterns.

The intangible aspects are more difficult to describe. These include what you've accomplished with family members, friends, colleagues, corporate family members, and all of your interpersonal relationships. This personal legacy of what you believed in represents the essence of who you really are. You have impacted individuals with your ideals, hopes, dreams, values, beliefs, and behavior patterns. They will remember your passion for them and for life in general. These men and women will be the ones who pass on truths about you to future generations.

A young clergyman, Dr. Martin Luther King, Jr., became an activist for the civil rights of African-Americans in the 1950s and 1960s. His efforts inspired a tremendous following of people who were eager for change in the culture of the United States. From boycotts to his famous "I Have a Dream" speech, Dr. King reinvigorated a movement for all human rights (Ling, 2002).

Despite his Nobel Peace Prize, Presidential Medal of Freedom, and Congressional Gold Medal, much of Dr. King's professional legacy exists in his passionate pursuit for transformation. "King contributed to greater consciousness of the black role in America...this message inhered primarily in his own person rather than in an enduring organization" (Gardner, 1995, p. 220). As Gardner points out, King really didn't need to build an organization or establish a constituency that would transcend his untimely death at the age of thirty-nine. Instead what he valued, believed in, and fought for "came to occupy a place in the country for which there had been no predecessor—and, for that matter, no successors" (p. 220).

Like many men and women throughout history, Dr. King's legacy has lasted and increased due to its inspiration and impact on others. As you consider "who" and "what" you truly value, take some time to reflect on a few questions about your lasting legacy:

+ Which individuals are most important in your life?
+ How and where do you invest in their lives? What impact do you hope to make on them?
+ When you're gone, what will they remember about you? Is there more to who you are that you've resisted sharing? Are there things about yourself that you want to change so that your legacy will reflect what you truly believe?
+ What kind of impact have you made on your family, friends, colleagues and corporate family members? What kind of story will they tell about you when you're no longer here?
+ What tangible legacy are you leaving behind for the next generation? Have you really accomplished all that you wanted to? What other plans, hopes, and dreams are yet to be fulfilled?
+ What about your intangible legacy? Have you inspired others in your life to do something bigger and better than you've done?

✦ If there was one phrase or saying that would summarize your life, what would it be? Would others say the same, or would their comments be different?

These questions, as well as many others, may take some time to work through, but the effort you make will impact the reality of the legacy you leave for future generations. Just like all of our straight line strategies, this unique approach to succession planning will offer you more satisfaction and fulfillment than you ever imagined! As we've said, *internal and intentional leadership development leads to a lasting legacy and legacy-building cannot happen without developing your skills at leading.*

> As we've said, internal and intentional leadership development leads to a lasting legacy and legacy-building cannot happen without developing your skills at leading.

THE PRESCRIPTION FOR SIGNIFICANT SUCCESS

So how does a hard-working leader like you meet the demands of the day in addition to acquiring all of the skill sets you need to attain the leading edge in life? With all that you've got on your calendar, can you really acquire leadership skills, equip your HPT with these Team Strategies, and have time enough left over to insure that you're indeed leaving a legacy?

We believe the answer is a most definite yes. The prescription for leaving a lasting legacy and achieving significant success has been carefully laid out for you through our "9 Straight Line Strategies." As we've explained, these nine tactics are straight-forward, but multi-faceted. They are attainable, but they will require time, effort, and energy to be fully implemented by you and all members of your corporate family. And we're confident that these strategies will help your organization become more productive and profitable, and both you and your HPT will experience more satisfaction and fulfillment about the work you are doing. We can almost guarantee that upon implementation, you will actually exceed your expectations.

Unlike some leadership development programs, our strategies are not merely theoretical—they're practical for everyday experiences in your organization. This type of practicality and execution is absolutely necessary for your ultimate success. If a pharmaceutical company merely talked about its amazing new medication, offered all sorts of details on the exciting chemical structure and potential physiological implications, but then never actually delivered a tangible product to the public, then there is no value, especially for the men and women who desperately needed that prescription! A prescription must be tangible, useable, and effective to be worth anything.

> **The principles are applicable, replicable, and sustainable.**

The same is true of our 9 Straight Line Strategies. These aren't simply good concepts that you've been reading about in *The Leading Edge* and now can file away on a shelf somewhere; *the principles are applicable, replicable, and sustainable.* But just like antibiotics, you can't decide to apply only four of the nine strategies and expect significant changes in your company; there is no multiple choice! Without taking the whole prescribed bottle, the infection will return. The specific protocol—application of all nine strategies to the best of your ability—will ensure optimum results.

But take note: just like modern-day medicines, the first prescription is not always 100% effective. Sometimes they've got to be adjusted a bit in order to battle a tough scenario. At other times the infection is resistant to the medicine, so a stronger course of action must be taken. That means as a leader you need to be realistic with your implementation of these strategies. You may have an extremely difficult case to confront in your current organization, so be prepared to fight the battle. *There's a good chance that you may encounter "resistance," especially when you're striving for the complete health of your corporate family!* What will ultimately make the difference is how you apply your strategic approach. It must be *internally* and *intentionally* implemented each and every day.

> There's a good chance that you may encounter "resistance," especially when you're striving for the complete health of your corporate family!

We are certain our prescription works because we've seen the results over and over again in leaders, their teams, and the organizations LEADon has worked with throughout the years. We'd like to share a few of these examples in the following sections.

A LEADER'S STORY

We met Steve right after he'd graduated from college. He had been hired by a large organization because of his terrific abilities and skills, but it was his passion, energy, and ideas about the future that immediately intrigued us. Steve enjoyed learning the principles that LEADon had been equipping his company's HPT with so much that he began to immerse himself in leadership literature during

> It must be internally and intentionally implemented each and every day.

his free time. Additionally, Steve continued taking courses to improve his skill sets in order to eventually lead others.

After many years of hard work, Steve decided to venture out and form his own company with two other colleagues. This wasn't an easy decision, especially since his former organization was growing and all forecasts pointed to their continued success. He had to choose between a comfortable position where he was financially secure and the uncertain prospects of an independent company where he could implement his own vision. In hindsight Steve took a tremendous chance with his career and financial security, but his gamble paid off big time. The reason he was so successful was because he'd taken the time to prepare for his leadership role and corresponding responsibilities far in advance. He had become well-acquainted with our straight line strategies for success, and he continued to utilize them with his new corporate family. Indeed, leadership development is a priority for him, his team, and his organization. He's now realizing the dream that he envisioned for his own career, and, most importantly, he's greatly impacting the lives of all members of his corporate family.

This Leader's Lasting Legacy: A strong, visionary company unique to its industry; an HPT that's being equipped for success through internal and intentional leadership development; a great personal and professional family whose members are empowered to strive for their own dreams based on his example.

A TEAM'S STORY

We met Doug, Joe, and Simon through a mutual business connection. Their architectural firm was already quite successful, but these leaders wanted to do more. They were committed to creating a unique culture that would stand the test of time.

These men also realized the benefit that internal and intentional leadership development would have on the productivity and profitability of their company. They appreciated the principle-based skill sets that LEADon emphasizes. These leaders made certain that the men and women of their organization would be fully equipped with these leadership skills.

There were three specific tactics that we implemented at Doug, Joe, and Simon's organization that allowed this process to operate successfully:

1. An Executive Team was formed that met at regular intervals in order to internally and intentionally learn and practice leadership skills themselves before they attempted to cascade them throughout the corporate family.
2. A Second Level Leadership Team was also formed. This was composed of present employees who fit the profile for future leadership and had the potential to become first-line executives in the future. These leaders had their own specific leadership meetings on a consistent basis.
3. Corporate Family gatherings are held regularly. The entire organization meets for rapport-building as well as cascading leadership skills.

Now, the company is more productive and profitable than ever. Doug, Joe, and Simon have opened an office in another city, and they've asked LEADon to begin the process of equipping the new corporate family members there with principle-based leadership skills. The team members in both offices are truly high-performing as evidenced by their continued strength.

This Team's Lasting Legacy: This High Performance Team has never been tighter as a group. There is unity, alignment and attunement, accountability, and mutual respect. The members of the HPT are growing the company, increasing productivity and profitability, and garnering a great reputation in a highly competitive market.

AN ORGANIZATION'S STORY

It didn't surprise us that Jay's organization was known for its unique Corporate Culture and was gaining respect not only in California, but also in many states where it was beginning to open new offices. Jay valued culture, and so did his organization. Based on this fact alone they attracted many entrepreneurial employees with visionary ideas and exemplary ideals. All of the leaders felt strongly about equipping the entire corporate family with the leadership skills needed to keep their business strong and competitive.

Jay was the type of leader who liked to spearhead programs that would complement his own style of leadership and equip current and future leaders. This was embraced by the founders of the company, so before long, LEADon was working with many of their key executives at various offices. Due to their passion for success, these leaders readily integrated the straight line strategies they were missing and began cascading them throughout their organization.

In order to push his organization to new heights of exceptional leadership, Jay continued to rally behind these leadership development efforts. He practiced these strategies himself, and he encouraged their development in everyone with whom he interacted. What kind of results did the organization experience due to all of this internal and intentional effort? Jay's company is stronger than ever.

This Organization's Lasting Legacy: Their name alone stands for quality in their industry. Many firms are now attempting to model their culture after Jay's company. Clients continue to see them as a "value buy," choosing to purchase their services rather than seek a discount that might save money, but not overall worth.

THE CONTINUING JOURNEY

Since the prescription for successful leadership involves implementing the 9 Straight Line Strategies that we've covered in *The Leading Edge*, let's take a few minutes to review them:

Chapter 2 - Straight Line #1:
Standards for Hall of Fame Leadership

Chapter 3 - Straight Line #2:
Six Benchmarks for Internal and Intentional Leadership

Chapter 4 - Straight Line #3:
Discover Personal and Professional Life Balance

Chapter 5 - Straight Line #4:
Field Your High Performance Team

Chapter 6 - Straight Line #5:
Develop Your High Performance Team

Chapter 7 - Straight Line #6:
Maintain Your High Performance Team

Chapter 8 - Straight Line #7:
Lead the Generations

Chapter 9 - Straight Line #8:
Corporate Culture Always Impacts the Bottom Line

Chapter 10 - Straight Line #9:
Leave a Lasting Legacy through Internal and Intentional Leadership

As a leader, which of these nine categories do you feel most competent in right now? Go down the list and mark which ones you could check off as progressing. Consider which strategies should be addressed next. Do you need assistance in this leadership development process? How are you assessing the results of these strategic approaches? Are you and your team members accountable to one another for the daily application of these principles?

This is a tremendous amount of information to process, but that's what exceptional leaders must do if they truly want to attain the leading edge in life. But, remember, you cannot do it all in a week, a month, or even in a year. Your organization took time to get where it is today, so you must allow for a season of growth, development, and more growth.

So, where do you begin? Here are a few suggestions:

+ Celebrate the successes you and your team have already experienced.
+ Prioritize the 9 Straight Line Strategies. What are the top three areas that you feel you and your team must work on now?
+ Set attainable goals and begin mentoring your HPT with those strategies.
+ Seek help to equip yourself with these skill sets and cascade them to your entire team.
+ Follow up with your HPT members. How are they feeling about the information they're learning?
+ Encourage HPT members to cascade these strategies to their "Sphere of Influence."
+ Once your top three strategies are in process, select one or two more to add to your new internal and intentional goals.

Remember, your organization will experience some successful seasons when you'll feel like you and your HPT don't need to do anything else to be productive and profitable. Other seasons will surprise you with an unexpected crisis or economic downturn, so don't be caught off guard! That's when you'll be thankful you took the time to work on these strategies even during the times that everything seemed so good. Perhaps you'll be even more astonished by exponential growth and the demands that this expansion places upon you and your corporate family. No matter what crosses your path in the journey ahead, learning and applying all nine of these straight line strategies will serve you well. Like the teams that train hard in the off season, you and your HPT will be ready for whatever life brings your way because you took the time, effort and energy to prepare yourselves today.

> You and your HPT will be ready for whatever life brings your way because you took the time, effort and energy to prepare yourselves today.

As the son of a famous founding father, John Quincy Adams was able to experience firsthand the trials, tribulations, and successes that come with leadership. He watched his father and his father's friends struggle in order to lead the American people to a better life. They had hopes, dreams, and plans for a great future, and they were willing to sacrifice everything if need be to attain them. His father influenced John Quincy not only through his personal life but also his professional one. No wonder John Adam's son was able to write the following words: "If your

> "If your actions inspire others to dream more, learn more, do more and become more, you are a leader."

actions inspire others to dream more, learn more, do more and become more, you are a leader."

Your leadership is making a difference in this world, one way or another. How you choose to apply the knowledge that you've acquired will profoundly impact how you lead those who are in your care. This journey is not for the impatient; it's for the industrious, the passionate, the committed, and the inspirational. You can improve your performance, both personally and professionally, through this intentional leadership process. So, keep going. Keep growing. Keep looking for the leading edge.

> Your leadership is making a difference in this world, one way or another.

SHARPENING YOUR EDGE

1. What will your legacy be when you are gone? If we were to audit your "Sphere of Influence," what would they say your legacy would be? Now that you still have time to consider it, what would you ideally like your legacy to be?

   Some of our clients have written out their own obituaries in order to sharpen their edge. Write out two to three paragraphs about what you'd like to have written about you when you're gone. How do you think others will remember who you were and what you've done? Do you like the thoughts you've written? Are there things that you'd like to change before it's too late?

2. What goals, hopes, dreams, and plans do you still want to accomplish in your personal and professional life? Write a list of these "yet-to-be-accomplished" thoughts, and post this along with a time-sensitive developmental plan so you can start these transformations today.

3. Who are you mentoring as part of your succession plan? If you don't have anyone, then start today by choosing leaders to be part of your specific coaching and mentoring efforts. Begin a program at work to cascade leadership skill sets to your entire corporate family.

4. Of all of the 9 Straight Line Strategies you've read about, which ones do you and your team have in place right now? Celebrate these in some way together this week! Which ones do you need to work on? Discuss these with your team, then devise a plan to begin sharpening your edge in these specific areas.

References

American Institute of Stress, The. (June, 2009). www.stress.org/job/htm.

Banks, J. (2001). *Cultural Diversity and Education: Foundations, Curriculum, and Teaching,* 4th Ed. Boston: Allyn & Bacon.

Benedict, R. (1934). *Patterns of Culture.* New York: The New American Library.

Blanchard, K. (1995). *Leadership and the One Minute Manager: Increasing Effectiveness Through Situational Leadership.* New York: William Morrow and Company, Inc.

Blayney, M. (2006). *Turning a Business Around: How to Spot the Warning Signs and Ensure a Business Stays Healthy,* 2nd Ed. New York: How to Books.

Brookhiser, R. (2008). *George Washington on Leadership.* New York: Basic Books.

Carleton, R.J., & Lineberry, C. (2001). *Achieving Post-Merger Success: A Stakeholder's Guide To Cultural Due Diligence.* San Francisco: Jossey-Bass/Pfeiffer.

Cherniss, C., & Goleman, D., Eds. (2001). *The Emotionally Intelligent Workplace: How to Select For, Measure, and Improve Emotional Intelligence in Individuals, Groups, And Organizations.* San Francisco: Jossey-Bass.

Chernow, R. (2004). *Titan: The Life of John D. Rockefeller.* New York: Vintage Books.

Cloud, H. (2006). *Integrity: The Courage to Meet the Demands of Reality.* New York: HarperCollins Publishers.

Coe, George A. (1925). *What Ails Our Youth?* New York: Charles Scribner's Sons.

Collins, J.C. (2001). *Good to Great: Why Some Companies Make the Leap...and Others Don't.* New York: HarperCollins Publishers.

Collins, J.C., & Porras, J.I. (1997). *Built to Last: Successful Habits of Visionary Companies.* New York: HarperCollins Publishers.

Covey, S.R. (1999). *Rethinking Stress.* www.franklincovey.com/organizatinal/serprod/rts.html.

Covey, S.R. (2007). *Work-Life Balance: A Different Cut.* FranklinCovery Co., www.Forbes.com.

Coyle, D. (2009). *The Talent Code: Greatness Isn't Born. It's Grown. Here's How.* New York: Bantam Books.

Deal, T.E., & Kennedy, A.A. (1982). *Corporate Cultures: The Rites and Rituals of Corporate Life.* New York: Addison-Wesley Publishing Company.

Denison, D. R. (1990) *Corporate Culture and Organizational Effectiveness: A Behavioral Approach to Financial Performance.* New Jersey: John Wiley & Sons.

Dive, B. (2004). *The Healthy Organization: A Revitalizing Approach to People and Management,* 2nd Ed. Philadelphia, PA: Kogan Page Publishers.

Ekman, J.P. & Friesen, W.V. (1978). *Facial Action Coding System, Part I and 2.* San Francisco: Human Interaction Laboratory, Dept. of Psychiatry, University of California.

Fankhauser, M. (July, 2009). *Coaching vs. Mentoring.* Center for Management and Organization Effectiveness. www.cmoe.com

Fullan, M. (2001). *Leading in a Culture of Change.* San Francisco: Jossey-Bass.

Fulmer, R.M., & Conger, J.A. (2004). *Growing Your Company's Leaders: How Great Organizations Use Succession Management to Sustain Competitive Advantage.* New York: AMACON.

Garcia, E. (2002). *Student Cultural Diversity: Understanding and Meeting the Challenge,* 3rd Ed. New York: Houghton Mifflin Company.

Gardner, H., & Laskin, E. (1995). *Leading Minds: An Anatomy of Leadership.* New York: Basic Books.

Gillon, S. (2004). *Boomer Nation: The Largest and Richest Generation Ever and How It Changed America.* New York: Free Press.

Gladwell, M. (2005). *Blink: The Power of Thinking Without Thinking.* New York: Back Bay Books.

Gladwell, M. (2008). *Outliers: The Story of Success.* New York: Little, Brown, and Company.

Glanz, B.A. (2002). *Handle with CARE: Motivating and Retaining Employees.* New York: McGraw-Hill.

Goleman, D. (1994). *Emotional Intelligence: Why It Can Matter More than IQ.* New York: Bantam Books.

Goleman, D., Boyatzis, R., & McKee, A. (2002). *Primal Leadership: Realizing the Power of Emotional Intelligence.* Boston: Harvard Business School Press.

Haughton, L. (2004). *It's Not What You Say…It's What You Do: How Following Through at Every Level Can Make or Break Your Company.* New York: Doubleday.

Hendricks, W. (1994). *The Manager's Role as Coach.* Shawnee Mission, KS: National Press Publications.

Hicks, R., & Hicks, K. (1999). *Boomers, Xers, and Other Strangers: Understanding the Generational Differences that Divide Us.* Wheaton, Illinois: Tyndale House Publishers.

Holtz, L. (2005). *Winning Every Day: The Game Plan for Success.* New York: Collins Business.

How Generations Work. (July, 2009). www.newworkforce.com.

Hutcheon, L. (2002). *Politics and Postmodernism,* 2nd ed. New York: Routledge.

Jenson, R. (2006). *Achieving Authentic Success: 10 Timeless Life Principles that will Maximize Your Real Potential.* Temecula, CA: Future Achievement International.

Koch, R. (2001). *The 80/20 Principle: The Secret to Achieving More with Less.* London: Nicholas Brealey Publishing.

Kotter, J.P., & Heskett, J.L. (1992). *Corporate Culture and Performance.* New York: Simon & Schuster.

Lancaster, L.C., & Stillman, D. (2002). *When Generations Collide: Who They Are, Why They Clash. How to Solve the Generational Puzzle at Work.* New York: Collins Business.

Lencioni, P. (2000). *The Four Obsessions of an Extraordinary Executive: A Leadership Fable.* San Francisco: Jossey-Bass.

Ling, P.J. (2002). *Martin Luther King, Jr.* United Kingdom: Routledge.

Loeppke, R., & Burton, W. (2003). *The Business Impact of Health and Health-Related Productivity.* Paper presented at the American Occupational Health Conference Joint Seminar #905, Atlanta World Congress Center.

MacLennan, N. (1995). *Coaching and Mentoring.* Great Britain: Gower Publishing House.

McCullough, D. (2001). *John Adams.* New York: Simon & Schuster.

McCullough, D. (2005). *1776.* New York: Simon & Schuster.

Marino, V. (2000, November 12). "It's All the Rage at Work, Too." *The New York Times, Money & Business,* p. 3.

McKinsey & Company, Inc., Koller, T., Goedhart, M., & Wessels, D. (2005). *Valuation: Measuring and Managing the Value of Companies,* 4th ed. New Jersey: John Wiley & Sons, Inc.

National Education Association, www.nea.org.

Newcott, B. (May—June 2009). Wisdom of the Elders. *AARP Magazine.* www.aarpmagaine.org.

Pascale, R., Millemann, M. & Gioja, L. (2000). *Surfing the Edge of Chaos.* New York: Crown Business Publishing.

Pfeffer, J. (1995). *Competitive Advantage through People.* Boston: Harvard Business School Press.

Pickens, T.B. (2008). *The First Billion is the Hardest: Reflections on a Life of Comebacks and America's Energy Future.* Largo, Maryland: Crown Business.

Raines, C. (2003). *Connecting Generations: The Sourcebook for a New Workplace.* Menlo Park, California: Crisp Publications.

Rosenbach, R.E., & Taylor, R.L. (2006). *Contemporary Issues in Leadership,* 6th ed. Boulder, Colorado: Westview Press.

Rothwell, W.J. (2009). *Effective Succession Planning: Ensuring Leadership Continuity and Building Talent from Within.* New York: AMACON.

Shipman, C., & Kay, K. (5/20/09). Women Will Rule Business. *Time* (On-line). www.time.com/time/specials/packages/article/ 0,28804,1898024.

Smith, J.W., & Churman, A.S. (1998). *Rocking the Ages: The Yankelovich Report on Generational Marketing.* New York: Harper Paperbacks.

Sorenson, T.C. (1996). *Kennedy.* New York: Bantam Books.

Torricelii, R. G. (2001). *Quotations for Public Speakers: A Historical, Literary, and Political Anthology.* New Jersey: Rutgers University Press.

Ukens, L.L. (2000). *Energize Your Audience: 75 Quick Activities that Get Them Started and Keep Them Going.* San Francisco: Jossey-Bass/Pfeiffer.

Wissler, C. (1923). *Man and Culture.* New York: Thomas Y. Crowell Company Publishers.

Zemke, R., Raines, C., & Filipczak, B. (2000). *Generations at Work: Managing the Clash of Veterans, Boomers, Xers, and Nexters in Your Workplace.* New York: American Management Association.